National Defense Research Institute

Aft and Fore

A Retrospective and Prospective Analysis of Navy Officer Management

Harry J. Thie ✦ **Margaret C. Harrell**

Jefferson P. Marquis ✦ **Kevin Brancato**

Roland J. Yardley ✦ **Clifford M. Graf II**

Jerry Sollinger

RAND

Prepared for the
United States Navy

Approved for public release; distribution unlimited

The research described in this report was conducted for the U.S. Navy within the Forces and Resources Policy Center of RAND's National Defense Research Institute, a federally funded research and development center supported by the Office of the Secretary of Defense, the Joint Staff, the unified commands, and the defense agencies under Contract DASW01-01-C-0004.

Library of Congress Cataloging-in-Publication Data

Aft and fore : a retrospective and prospective analysis of Navy officer management /
    Harry J. Thie ... [et al.].
        p. cm.
    "MR-1479."
    Includes bibliographical references.
    ISBN 0-8330-3270-4
    1. United States. Navy—Officers. 2. United States. Navy—Personnel
management. I. Thie, Harry.

    VB313 .A66 2002
    359.3'3'0973—dc21

                                                                    2002031845

RAND is a nonprofit institution that helps improve policy and decisionmaking through research and analysis. RAND® is a registered trademark. RAND's publications do not necessarily reflect the opinions or policies of its research sponsors.

Published 2003 by RAND
1700 Main Street, P.O. Box 2138, Santa Monica, CA 90407-2138
1200 South Hayes Street, Arlington, VA 22202-5050
201 North Craig Street, Suite 202, Pittsburgh, PA 15213-1516
RAND URL: http://www.rand.org/
To order RAND documents or to obtain additional information,
contact Distribution Services: Telephone: (310) 451-7002;
Fax: (310) 451-6915; Email: order@rand.org

The Manpower, Personnel, and Training section of the Assessments Division of the Deputy Chief of Naval Operations for Resources, Warfare Requirements, and Assessments asked RAND to review past and present officer management practices, assess the ability of the Navy to meet its authorizations for officers, and examine likely future needs for officers and changes in their management. We were asked to make our assessment as data-based as possible.

This research reviews the evolution of policy and the management of the officer corps as a basis for discerning trends and cycles in requirements and inventory of officers that may need to be accommodated in the future. It also identifies where mismatches between authorizations and inventory exist as well as the costs of such gaps. The research identifies dynamic factors affecting officer requirements for unrestricted line, restricted line, and staff corps and identifies the past, present, and future officer manpower requirement in response to such factors. Moreover, this research outlines the officer personnel structure designed to support the requirement; examines the gaps and excesses resulting from existing accession, development, and transitioning processes; and proposes methods to provide better support to the future force structure.

This report describes the results of the research and should be of interest to the defense manpower and personnel community. The project has a large scope—past, present, and future, by community and grade, for both requirements and inventory of naval officers. In particular, the data within this document represent a resource for manpower and personnel planners. This work is both broad in scope—it includes historical observations about Navy manpower as well as current manning gaps and cost implications—and detailed in the modeling approach used and the policy implications discussed.

This research was conducted for the United States Navy within the Forces and Resources Policy Center of RAND's National Defense Research Institute, a federally funded research and development center sponsored by the Office of the Secretary of Defense, the Joint Staff, the unified commands, and the defense agencies.

CONTENTS

FIGURES

TABLES

The Navy recently examined its officer structure with an eye toward determining how well it can meet current and future demands. It was particularly interested in gaps between the supply of and demand for officers and the potential costs of such gaps. Of equal interest was how demands might change in the future and whether the current system for managing officers—accession, development, assignment, promotion, and, ultimately, separation—would satisfy tomorrow's requirements.

The Navy asked RAND's National Defense Research Institute (NDRI) to assist and, more specifically, for

- an analysis of the documents—studies, statutes, and policies—that influence personnel authorizations and inventory and for a catalogue of the changes in both over the past 20 years.

- a comparison between authorizations and inventory and an analysis of the cost of any differences.

- an estimate on the personnel requirements for 2010 and 2017.

The purpose of these estimates was not to determine specific requirements. Rather, it was to assess the adequacy of officer personnel management practices to manage the types of structures that would exist then.

THE GAPS

We refer to any difference between authorization and inventory as a "gap." Navy personnel managers frequently use different terms, such as deltas, mismatches, and differences. Many tend to view a gap only as a difference between authorizations and inventory at the aggregate level of a community or the officer corps. Our use of gaps refers not only to these situations but also to differences in grade or skill. Gaps can be either overages or shortages of inventory compared with authorizations.

Any investigation into the gaps between authorizations and officers assigned must examine specialties rather than the officer corps as a whole because gaps occur in different communities for different reasons. For example, the system can respond to large-scale changes most easily at the junior grades. It is far easier simply to access or stop accessing additional officers than it is to correct imbalances at, say, the O-4 level (although not necessarily less expensive). But making large-scale changes among the junior grades results in officer cohorts of different sizes moving through the system, which engenders complex management problems later on.

Other influences can also affect gaps. Nurses provide an example of how external constraints can cause gaps. The Nurse Corps lacks a history of senior officers because, before 1967, women generally could not be promoted beyond O-4. Therefore, they tended either to retire at O-4 or to leave the service before becoming O-3s. The Navy revisited the policy in the late 1980s and opened up more field-grade assignments to nurses. However, because field-grade billets were limited as a matter of law, any additional nurse promotions would come at the expense of some other community, and the Navy did not create enough billets to avoid promotion stagnation, even though nurses were receiving a reasonable share of promotions.

Grade structures of individual communities can also contribute to gaps. For example, the inventory of doctors at the O-5 and O-6 levels has exceeded authorizations since the early 1990s. Analysis of the grade structure shows high authorizations for O-3s and O-4s. The senior grades do not have enough authorizations to absorb the junior grades as they get promoted, leading to overages at the senior grades.

THE COST OF GAPS

Gaps create two types of costs: hard and soft. *Hard costs* are the most straightforward and include dollar costs of acquiring, paying, and training officers. *Soft costs* are more nebulous but nonetheless real. They include such elements as lower productivity due to low morale or readiness problems that result from unfinished work or low retention.

Gaps can have positive or negative hard-cost implications. If a community is understaffed relative to authorizations, savings accrue. If overstaffed, then the Navy incurs costs. These costs and savings vary by community. The costs of overages in senior doctors are relatively more expensive than, say, overages among junior supply officers. An O-3 pilot is estimated to cost about a third more than an O-3 surface warfare officer (SWO). An O-6 doctor costs more than an O-6 SWO but less than an O-6 submariner.[1] Current Navy practice does not take these differential costs into account in its planning and programming procedures, but it should.

Soft costs also occur when the system is out of balance. An excess of junior officers and a shortage of senior officers might lead to more junior personnel occupying senior positions or carrying out the duties de facto without the seasoning and experience to perform them well or without the recognition of being in the position, although they would potentially benefit from having greater responsibility. Thus, job performance suffers, and the morale of the junior officers may also decline because of lower job satisfaction and resentment over carrying out responsibilities without being compensated fairly. The reverse situation—too few junior officers— can be equally poor, with senior officers stretched thin and carrying out duties normally performed by junior personnel (e.g., standing watch).

Most communities have various overages and shortages by grade, but in general the costs and savings offset each other. However, this is not true for all communities. For example, the cost of the surface warfare community has increased steadily since about 1993, meaning that inventory has consistently exceeded authorizations, largely at the junior grades. While junior officers are less expensive, when the number of overages becomes substantial, costs get quite high.

---

[1]Cost differences were calculated using the Navy COMET (Cost of Manpower Estimating Tool) model.

Intelligence officer billets have historically been staffed at less than authorized.

The cost differentials have important implications for how the Navy staffs its communities and uses its different officers. For example, it is expensive to have overages in aviators and submariners. Similarly, overstaffing joint billets with aviators and submarine officers, which the Navy tends to do, is relatively more expensive than staffing them with SWOs.[2] Indeed, the aviation community is far and away the most expensive in the Navy. Each aviator is costly—and there are many. Given the cost differences among communities, the Navy should always seek to replace higher-cost personnel with lower-cost personnel, all other things being equal. Also, in bringing inventory and authorizations into line, the aviation community would be a good place to start because of its relative size (50 percent of the unrestricted line community) and the cost of training and compensating each aviator.

The Navy must review its costs and savings by community and grade. In the past, the Navy has saved dollars by persistent understaffing. However, that trend has reversed, and costs have climbed as inventory has moved toward authorizations. Unknown at this point is whether the short-term dollar costs of minimizing gaps will ultimately be offset by the reduction in soft costs that could lead to future savings through such effects as increased retention.

FUTURE REQUIREMENTS

To gain some insight into how the personnel system might have to respond in the future and its ability to do so, we developed two scenarios: one for 2010 and another for 2017. Factors that will affect the shape of the future officer corps include changes in force structure, doctrine, organizations, emerging technologies, joint activities, and

---

[2]This assumes that the Navy would need to "grow" fewer aviators or submariners if there were not a consistent use of them in the joint community. If community managers are placing them there because they have an excess of senior officers propagated by the current system that does not—in part due to legal restrictions—manage to requirements, then placing these officers in joint assignments is not costly because of sunk cost. This assumption is addressed later in this report as we recommend managing officers to requirements, provided relief is given from such constraints as the Defense Officer Personnel Management Act (DOPMA).

training procedures. These scenarios, to include the force structure and other assumptions, are described in greater detail in the body of this report. The text below summarizes the scenarios.

The 2010 Navy

The 2010 Navy remains essentially stable compared with the Navy of today, but some changes occur. Force structure and organizational changes, adoption of innovations, and continuing base realignment efforts will alter the shape of the officer corps. The effect will vary by community. For example, force structure changes, or the expected changes in the numbers and types of platforms and personnel assigned to them, will have the greatest effect on submarine and limited duty officers (LDOs) by reducing their numbers. Organizational streamlining will effect reductions across most unrestricted line officer specialties. Special warfare officers increase in number in response to mission needs, and restricted line billets will increase largely in response to administrative changes.

The 2017 Navy

The Navy, acutely aware of its need for transformation, also realizes that the process will not be rapid. Even by 2017, about two-thirds of the fleet will include ships and aircraft from the present era. However, additional force structure and organization changes will occur between 2000 and 2017, and the Navy will have adopted additional technologies and developed different functions. Overall, the number of officers will decline as a result of streamlining organizations, adopting technologies, outsourcing work, and shifting some functions to the enlisted force.

The upshot of the various influences will be a smaller, more skilled, more experienced (and thus more senior), more specialized, and more joint officer corps. The emphasis in the officer corps will shift from operating platforms to integrating them. Unrestricted line officers will continue to be in demand, and a new community will emerge to meet the need for broad warfare expertise. Staff officers ashore will decline in numbers as outsourcing and privatization take some functions out of the Navy. Demand for restricted line officers will hold steady but will increase for some technical communities as well as for LDOs and chief warrant officers.

WHAT THE FUTURE IMPLIES FOR OFFICER MANAGEMENT

The prime purpose of the two future scenarios is not to establish requirements. Rather, it is to test the flexibility of existing management tools and to explore what policy changes might be necessary to respond to the types of changes outlined in our scenarios.

In broad terms, the Navy's officer management system needs to be more strategic, more systemic, less uniform, and more flexible. By "strategic," we mean that it needs to be a more active instrument in developing the Navy's overall future strategy. Put another way, the Navy should be trying to shape the size and composition of the officer corps so that it is structured to meet future missions rather than reacting to past changes in the internal and external environment, which is what it largely does now.

Officer management should work as a system. Accession is not a separate function from retention and retirement. The process of bringing officers into the service and educating, promoting, assigning, developing, and separating them is interlinked. The process has to be internally consistent, yet needs to answer the needs of multiple stakeholders. Above all, managers must recognize that changes in one functional area can ripple throughout the system.

The issue of uniformity relates to the current practice of a centralized approach to officer management that best suits the Navy's dominant officer occupations. That approach may not work well for other occupations, and thus the question arises of whether they should be managed differently. Our judgment is that, if it is to prosper in increasingly complex environments, the Navy may need to adopt a more specialized approach.

Finally, it may be that change is the only constant, and whatever system the Navy adopts should be flexible enough to react to that change. Imbuing a system with flexibility to accommodate inevitable change may mean fewer centralized policies and controls. More flexibility carries with it such increased risk as diminished Navy identity and increased rivalry among groups.

RECOMMENDATIONS

We suggest that the Navy

- Manage communities individually, flexibly employing such tools as longer careers and broader promotion zones as needed to align inventory and authorizations. This would require the Navy to seek legislative relief from DOPMA.

- Acknowledge that the grade structure for some communities (e.g., submarine, intelligence) is insupportable and either restructure it or employ management tools that will enable the Navy to meet the requirements.

- Restructure the management of LDOs so that they are managed within the communities they associate with.

- Consider manpower costs by community and grade when planning for and filling requirements. Using a homogenized average manpower cost in the planning process obscures the true costs and leads to expensive assignment policies.

- Recognize that recruiting and training fewer officers initially but using such incentives as better promotion opportunity to keep them longer may be considerably more cost-effective.

- Consider establishing communities that can accommodate likely force structure changes and technological advances—e.g., network-centric warfare.

ACKNOWLEDGMENTS

The authors thank the staff of the Navy N81 office for their support, particularly Richard Robbins, CDR Keith Kowalski, LCDR Thomas Keane, and Linda Jo Graham. We also thank numerous people who provided data and shared their own analysis or expertise. Dawn DeIongh, Alex Sinaiko, and Don Rice of the Defense Manpower Data Center were extremely helpful providing data sources. We also appreciate the assistance of CDR William Hatch (Naval Postgraduate School) and of RAND colleagues Robert Emmerichs, Roger Brown, Charles Kaylor, and Ray Conley. This report benefited from the careful reviews of RAND colleagues John Schrader and Irving Blickstein. We also thank Phillip Wirtz and Stephen Bloodsworth in publicatons for integrating the elements of the report into their final form.

ABBREVIATIONS

AEDO	Aerospace engineering duty officer
AIR	Aviator (community)
AMD	Activity Manpower Document
BA	Billets Authorized
BRAC	Base Realignment and Closure
C4I	Command, control, communications, computers, and intelligence
CBO	Congressional Budget Office
CEC	Civil Engineer Corps
CNA	Center for Naval Analyses
CNO	Chief of Naval Operations
COB	Current onboard
COMET	Cost of Manpower Estimating Tool
COMNAVSURFLANT	Commander, Naval Surface Force, U.S. Atlantic Fleet
CRYPTO	Cryptologic (community)
CVBG	Carrier Battle Group
CWO	Chief warrant officer
DAWIA	Defense Acquisition Workforce Improvement Act

DFAS	Defense Finance and Accounting Service
DMDC	Defense Manpower Data Center
DMRR	Defense Manpower Requirements Report
DoD	Department of Defense
DOPMA	Defense Officer Personnel Management Act
EDO	Engineering duty officer
EDVR	Enlisted Distribution Verification Report
EOD	Explosive ordnance disposal
FMD	Fleet Manpower Document
FQ	Fully qualified
FSO	Fleet support officer
FY	Fiscal year
FYDP	Future Years Defense Program
GAO	General Accounting Office
GNFPP	Global Naval Force Presence Policy
Goldwaters-Nichols	Goldwaters-Nichols Department of Defense Reorganization Act of 1986
HR	Human resources
Intel	Intelligence (community)
IP	Information professional
JAG	Judge Advocate General
LDO	Limited duty officer
MCM	Mine countermeasures
MPN	Military Personnel, Navy

NMP	Navy Manning Plan
NWI	Naval warfare integrator
O&S	Operations and support
OCEANO	Oceanographer (community) `
ODCR	Officer Distribution Control Report
OGLA	Officer Grade Limitation Act
OPA	Officer Programmed Authorization
OSD	Office of the Secretary of Defense
PAO	Public affairs officer (community)
PERSTEMPO	Personnel tempo
POR	Program of Record
RL	Restricted line (officer)
RQMTS	Wartime requirements
SELRES	Selected reservists
SMD	Ship Manpower Document
SPECOPS	Special operations
SPECWAR	Special warfare
SQMD	Squadron Manpower Document
SUB	Submariner (community)
SWO	Surface warfare officer
TYCOM	Type commander
UAV	Unmanned aerial vehicle
UIC	Unit Identification Code
URL	Unrestricted line (officer)
VAMOSC	Visibility and Management of Operating and Support Costs
YOS	Years of service

Chapter One

INTRODUCTION

BACKGROUND

The Navy must enter, develop, and retain an officer corps of approximately 55,000 for the foreseeable future. Although the total number of officers will probably not change significantly, the composition of the officer force may change considerably because of changes in the operational force structure and other internal and external factors. To support potential changes in officer requirements, the Navy must analyze long-range strategies to manage the various officer communities. The present personnel management framework may not be an adequate structure for the future.

RESEARCH OBJECTIVES

We have five primary objectives in this research. First, we were asked to analyze relevant studies, policy, and statutes that influence officer requirements and personnel structures. We did this by reviewing past RAND studies and other relevant research, by reviewing Title 10 U.S. Code for officer management, and by interviewing with knowledgeable policy experts.

Second, we were asked to catalogue changes to officer authorizations for the past 20 years and changes to officer personnel structures for a period of at least that long. The catalogue was to be built at the level of detail of grade, occupation, and experience. As part of this cataloguing, we were asked to outline and discuss ratios that have been used to assess the officer force, such as enlisted-to-officer and tooth-to-tail. To accomplish this major task, we drew on data from a variety of sources, including the Defense Manpower Data Center (DMDC), the Center for Naval Analyses (CNA), the Directorate for Information Operations and Reports in the Office of the Secretary of Defense (OSD), and various published materials. We used past RAND reports, published materials, and the experience and knowledge of the research team.

Third, we were asked to compare officer authorizations and inventory to identify gaps—also referred to as deltas, differences, and mismatches—between the two. We discuss the hard and soft costs of these gaps and estimate their dollar costs.

The last two research objectives look to the future. What are the likely requirements for officers in the years 2010 and 2017? What officer management practices are needed in these future time periods to minimize any likely gaps between authorizations and inventory? We accomplish the former task by applying trend, cycle, and the likely effects of internal and external factors to existing authorizations to get future estimates of them. We accomplish the latter task through the use of system dynamics models applied to officer structures to determine which practices might need to change.

DATA SOURCES

Completing our objectives required the acquisition of accurate historical authorization and inventory numbers. The following datasets and documents were the subject matter of the second and third objectives and were the basis for objectives four and five.

The official numbers of end-strength authorizations come from Officer Programmed Authorizations (OPAs). OPAs are published at the end of every fiscal year. Each report contains a single year of historical and five years of forecasted authorizations by grade and designator. An OPA database was constructed covering 1980–2000 by manually entering the reports from 1980, 1985, 1990, 1995, and 2000.

The historical figures from these years were compared with two electronic authorization databases—one obtained from DMDC and the other from CNA. Both datasets detail annual authorizations by grade, designator, unit, subspecialty, and additional qualification.

While both were comparable, the CNA dataset was used for almost all analyses because of its greater fidelity to the OPA. The DMDC billet file was used for tooth-to-tail analysis because unlike the CNA dataset, it contained program element codes, permitting analysis by resource category.

Our inventory file was also provided by CNA. Manning levels of select designators and grades were compared to a monthly PERS-TEMPO dataset, and were sufficiently close to permit serious analysis.

Proper use of these datasets required documentation of dataset-specific coding, as well as codes constructed by the Navy and the Department of Defense (DoD). All Navy Unit Identification Codes (UICs) were translated by a master UIC file obtained from the Defense Finance and Accounting Service (DFAS). All Program Element Codes were translated by document DoD 7045.7-H, *FYDP Program Structure*. All other codes were translated from the *Total Force Manpower Management System (TFMMS) Coding Directory* and the *Manual of Navy Officer Manpower and Personnel Classifications*, NAVPERS 15839I, Volumes I and II.

MANPOWER TERMINOLOGY USED IN THE REPORT

Figure 1.1 establishes some of the terminology used in this report. We use Navy definitions for various terms. The figure distinguishes manpower ("spaces") terms from personnel ("faces") terminology. Requirements are the wartime requirements established in the Ship Manpower Document (SMD), the Squadron Manpower Document (SQMD), and the Fleet Manpower Document (FMD). Billets Authorized (BA) are the share of requirements that are funded, as indicated in the Activity Manpower Document (AMD). On the personnel side, the Navy Manning Plan (NMP) is the "fair share" distribution plan intended to man units based on the inventory of personnel available and is a determination of the most equitable level of manning an activity can expect on the basis of predicted manpower assets. Commands normally expect to be manned at NMP levels rather than at BA levels. NMP includes personnel actually assigned to a unit, as specified in the Officer Distribution Control Report (ODCR). Because

RAND*MR1479-1.1*

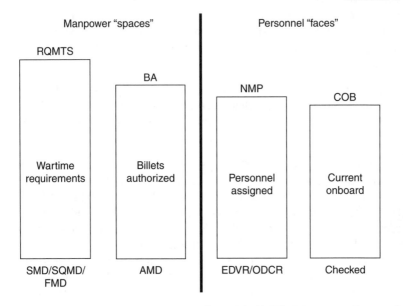

SOURCE: Adapted from Naval Postgraduate School, "The Manpower, Personnel, and Training Course," Manpower Requirements Module, June 20, 2001.

Figure 1.1—Manpower Definitions

of lags in the personnel assignment system and absences for personal reasons or extended period of temporary duty, current onboard (COB) is a subset of the NMP, and it reflects those individuals who have been assigned to and have checked into a unit. For the most part, we refer to billets authorized as "authorizations" and the NMP as "inventory." While some of the historical data may not use these exact terms, they are sufficient for the level of detail we are working at.

ORGANIZATION OF THE REPORT

This report contains eight chapters. The next two chapters include background material for those interested in the broader issue of officer career management: Chapter Two addresses the laws, policies, and initiatives relevant to officer requirements and management, and Chapter Three provides a historical analysis of the officer corps and requirements for it. Nonetheless, those readers interested primarily in the analysis of the current Navy manpower system and policy implications for the future may want to skip ahead to Chapter Four, which addresses the gaps between officer authorizations and inventory. Chapter Five discusses costs of these gaps, both financial and others. Chapter Six derives possible future requirements as a basis for assessing personnel management practices. Chapter Seven addresses the challenges such needs pose for those who manage officer inventory. Chapter Eight offers observations and recommendations.

Chapter Two

LAWS, POLICIES, AND INITIATIVES RELEVANT TO OFFICER MANAGEMENT

Before World War II, there was a Department of the Navy and a Department of War. The two departments and their officers were treated differently from one another by Congress in terms of pay, promotion, survivor benefits (for Army), and in myriad other ways. For a long time, the Army had generals, but the Navy had no officers of flag rank.

Navy officership paralleled the British system, while Army officership was based more on militia concepts. Between the time of the Mexican War and World War I, more than 50 percent of naval officers were sons of the professional and merchant classes: bankers, manufacturers, judges, merchants, congressmen, lawyers, diplomats, etc. For a similar period, less than 31 percent of Army officers of these disciplines entered service. All naval officers eventually came from the academy—which was founded in 1845. West Point, founded earlier in 1809, did not have a similar monopoly on officer accessions.

The naval officer corps developed in ship-to-shore mode. Originally, officers were only paid while they were on ships. Later, partial pay was granted while they were on shore awaiting ships. Eventually, given partial pay, officers were required to do shore work. The concept of naval officers doing shore work evolved over time and did not necessarily result from conscious policy choices. In 1902, there were requirements for 1,206 line officers assigned to ships, 264 to shore jobs, and 60 in an individuals account.[1] Excluding the individuals account there was a sea/shore ratio of 4.6 to 1; with the individuals account, it was 3.7 to 1.

Throughout naval officer history, there has been an internecine fight as to who would be included in the line. Typically, it was the quarterdeck officer verses a series of emerging specialties: engineers, surgeons, chaplains, ship constructors, and naval architects. Some were eventually amalgamated into the line as their own communities disappeared. Some eventually were considered line. Others have never been. There was also long-standing controversy over the means for managing the officer corps. Some advocated equity, in which seniority ruled, especially with respect to promotions. Others argued for efficiency, in which some seniority protections were taken away from individuals through the workings of "plucking boards" to free up promotions for others. Chisholm has identified 1916 as the year in which the shift from equity to efficiency occurred in the Navy and where service needs were placed ahead of individual prerogatives.[2]

This chapter reviews legislation, studies, policies, and initiatives that influence officer personnel structure and requirements.

OFFICER PERSONNEL MANAGEMENT: DEVELOPING THE PRESENT FRAMEWORK

Before 1916, officer personnel management was piecemeal and functional and usually subordinated service needs to officer prerogatives. Problems were addressed periodically that dealt with accessing, promoting, and separating officers, but seldom did policymakers focus on developing officers, that is, training, educating, and broadening their experience.

Different solutions for common problems were proffered for the War Department and the Department of the Navy. A Naval Academy was debated for years. A Naval School was finally established on a 10-acre

---

[1]Personnel not filling programmed manpower structure spaces are in the individuals account. This includes transients, trainees, patients, prisoners, holders, cadets, and students.

[2]Chisholm (2001).

Army post in Annapolis in 1845 and became the Naval Academy in 1850, upholding a curriculum requiring midshipmen to study at the Academy for four years and to train aboard ships each summer. A more universal program of training prospective officers prior to entry did not exist until just before World War I.

Promotion was the most vehemently argued function over the years, in terms of both uniform application to different occupations (which officers should be promoted) and the workings of the seniority system. In the Navy, promotion was based purely on seniority until the early 1900s, and in the Army, not until after World War II. Everyone got promoted—you just had to wait your turn. A history of naval officer management from 1793 to 1941 is entitled, not surprisingly, *Waiting for Dead Men's Shoes* (Chisholm, 2001). Moreover, until the 1870s, the only way to leave the service was to quit, die, or become disabled. The idea of retirement took hold after the Civil War as a means to leave service with an old-age pension.

For much of the past 50 years, a consensus has existed within the defense policy community to structure the size of the officer corps such that it would supply the appropriate number of officers from all of the services for both wartime and peacetime requirements. The role the United States played in World War II and in the early Cold War convinced Congress that, in spite of a very large demobilization, there was a "continuing need for many thousands of temporary officers for years into the future." Congress provided a permanent career plan for Regular Army and Regular Naval officers, and yet, at the same time, authority was provided for carrying along 30,000–40,000 temporary officers for some years. Congress's hope was that it would reduce the officer corps over the course of the decade following World War II.

In the Officer Personnel Act of 1947, Congress imposed tight controls on permanent promotions but none over temporary promotions in the Army and Air Force and only limited ones over temporary promotions in the Navy and Marine Corps. In response to a growing concern over temporary promotions and the number of officers holding high grade, Congress established grade limitations through amendments to the budget and in 1954 passed the Officer Grade Limitation Act (OGLA), which imposed statutory limitations on the number of regular and reserve officers who could serve in the grades of lieutenant commander and above (and other service equivalents).

Despite these efforts, the number of senior officers continued to grow disproportionately as large Korean War accession cohorts aged (particularly in the Air Force), necessitating annual grade relief legislation. This problem was compounded in the "hollow military" era of the 1970s by the difficulty in retaining promising junior officers. Ultimately, Congress responded with the Defense Officer Personnel Management Act (DOPMA) of 1980, which reformed the jury-rigged system of active and reserve officer commissions and grade controls that had emerged since the end of World War II. Among other things, DOPMA provided that the number of officers allowed in each service in grades O-4 to O-6 be determined annually by the grade table, based on total officer end strength. In addition, DOPMA did away with separate temporary and permanent promotion systems, provided that all active-duty officers would become regular officers after 11 years of service, and declared that regular officers could not be involuntarily separated after five years of service, unless they had failed consecutively to be selected for promotion.

In sum, DOPMA provided many tools to "grow" the officer corps, but it made the involuntary separation of career officers more difficult. This did not seem to be a problem during the period of the Reagan military buildup of the early 1980s, given the high demand for more (and more highly graded) commissioned officers. Under DOPMA rules, the increased end strength (made up of mostly junior officers) instantaneously increased the number of allowable field-grade officers.[3] As a result, the DOPMA system treated company-grade[4] and field-grade officers in service at the start of the Reagan buildup to a windfall as promotion opportunities rose and as the time between promotions decreased. However, these higher levels of promotion opportunity and shorter promotion cycles could be maintained only if officer end strength were allowed to stay high or grow indefinitely—a situation that did not come to pass.

---

[3]We use "field grade" in this report to refer to officers in paygrades O-4 to O-6. They are also referred to as "controlled grade." Greatly simplified, DOPMA sets the allowable number of field-grade officers as a percentage of the total number of officers.

[4]"Company grade" includes officers in paygrades O-1 to O-3.

Faced with the general drawdown in U.S. military forces at the end of the Cold War, DoD found it increasingly difficult in the late 1980s to meet end strength and grade-table limits and adhere to reasonable promotion opportunities and timing while remaining within the tenure constraints imposed by DOPMA. The voluntary early-out program, early retirement boards, and other DOPMA-authorized tools proved insufficient to reduce the force in a balanced way as quickly or deeply as proposed. As a result, Congress agreed to ease DOPMA rules to permit the involuntary separation of officers, beginning with the FY 1991 National Defense Authorization Act, which permitted the Secretary of Defense (during a five-year period) to shorten the period of selective continuation, expand selective early retirement, and convene selection boards to discharge regular officers. The FY 1992 and FY 1993 National Defense Authorization Acts further enhanced the services' ability to "shape" the force through involuntary separation—albeit only after offering servicemembers a choice of two voluntary incentive programs.[5]

Since the early 1990s, DOPMA's inflexibility in managing the post–Cold War reduction of the military has come under criticism. DOPMA forces a choice among grade-table violations (law), diminution of proffered tenure (law), or proffered promotion opportunity/timing (policy, promise).[6] In general, the solution chosen was a further loosening of the DOPMA rules, particularly to overcome problems created by the instantaneous nature of the grade tables.

The relative merits of uniformity and specialization have been at the heart of the debate over managing the composition of the officer corps in the postwar period. As they struggled to create a permanent military establishment in the early years of the Cold War, key defense reformers in Congress and the administration were guided by two major impressions drawn from World War II: (1) the senior military leadership, particularly in the Army, had largely lacked the vigor and

---

[5]Voluntary Separation Incentive and Special Separation Benefit.

[6]There is a mathematical relationship among the number in grade, the length of time spent in grade, the speed of advancement to a grade, and the number promoted to that grade. With the number in grade governed by law (with the exception of medical doctors and dentists), the other policy goals cannot be met because people choose to stay longer, the end strength comes down, or both.

creativity necessary to lead U.S. forces in the opening days of the war,[7] and (2) conflicts between senior leadership in the Army and Navy had prolonged the conflict longer than was necessary and had cost American lives.

To a great extent, these two impressions influenced significant provisions of the Officer Personnel Act (1947) and National Security Act (1947), which in different ways stressed the need for greater uniformity among the services. To maintain a young and vigorous officer corps, the Officer Personnel Act provided that the Navy's "up-or-out" officer promotion system would be extended (up to a point) to the Army and Air Force; tenure of a "successful" regular officer career in all services would be set for officers below flag rank at 30 years; and voluntary retirement could take place upon reaching 20 years of commissioned service.[8] For its part, the National Security Act created a more unified national military establishment with a Secretary of Defense at the top and a Joint Chiefs of Staff serving as a military advisory committee to the Secretary and the President.

Displeased with the incompleteness of the 1940s-era defense reforms—as well as what some considered a string of strategic and operational failures in Korea and Vietnam (1950s–1960s) and in Iran and Grenada (1970s–1980s)—defense experts, military personnel, and politicians alike began arguing for a greater focus on military professionalism and joint operations. Along with the move to an all-voluntary military and increased benefits and recognition for military service, the objective of a more professional, combat-ready military was met by an improved up-or-out promotion system for officers, with common promotion, separation, and retirement rules

---

[7]General Eisenhower, as Army Chief of Staff, told Congress that with few exceptions those who held senior command positions before World War II "had to be replaced and gotten out of the way and younger men had to come along and take over the job"(Hearings Before the Senate Committee on Armed Services, 1947, p. 1).

[8]OGLA had one other provision of note. Concerned about too many officers voluntarily retiring (at half pay) at the 20-year mark, Congress set limits on voluntary retirements (the Van Zandt Amendment) in the 1954 Defense Appropriations Act. Assuring Congress during hearings on OGLA that there would be no wholesale retirements in returning to unrestricted 20-year departures ("It is probable that, in the future, the privilege of voluntary retirement after completion of 20 or more years of service will be exercised little. . . ."), the military services won repeal of the restriction in Section 402 of OGLA. The services' predictions at the time that most successful officers would pursue a full 30-year career proved to be off the mark.

for all services. As laid out in DOPMA (1980), the "up" portion of the up-or-out system provided that, in general, officers would move through the system in "cohorts" originally determined by the year of commissioning and would compete for promotion to the next highest grade against other members of the group at set years-of-service points. The "out" portion of the up-or-out system provided that fully qualified officers "twice passed over for promotion, after a certain number of years, depending upon their particular grade, were to be separated from active service, and if eligible retired." In 1991, legislation similar for DOPMA was approved for managing warrant officers to include similar provisions for separating these technical specialists for failure of promotion, even if fully qualified.

The movement to improve the joint operations capability of the military culminated in the Goldwater-Nichols Department of Defense Reorganization Act of 1986, which revised and clarified the DoD operational chain of command and Joint Chiefs of Staff functions and responsibilities (Title I); assigned the Chairman of the Joint Chiefs of Staff the role of chief military advisor (Title II); and established a joint officer specialty occupational category and personnel policies to provide incentives and attract officers to joint-duty assignments (Title IV). Whereas the overall intent of Goldwater-Nichols was to create greater unity within DoD, the effect of Title IV was to foster the development of a new class of officers, specializing in joint operations, whose career pattern diverged from the typical line officer.

The trend toward officer specialization was also evinced by the passage of the Defense Acquisition Workforce Improvement Act (DAWIA) in 1990. Faced with a series of highly publicized defense-related procurement scandals in the 1980s—as well as an apparently diminishing lead over the Soviet Union in important areas of military technology—a majority in Congress became convinced that the skills and training of the professional warrior were inadequate for the job of acquiring sophisticated weaponry and support equipment. What was needed was a separate corps of acquisition professionals who, with education and training in acquisition, devoted most of their careers to acquisition. DAWIA fulfilled this aim by establishing an Acquisition Corps for the various components of DoD, centralizing acquisition training management under a new Defense Acquisition

University, and creating distinct career fields (e.g., program management, acquisition logistics) within the Acquisition Corps.

Responding to the Revolution in Business Affairs in the 1980s and 1990s and stimulated by advances in information technology— as well as the corresponding Reinventing Government initiative— studies by the Defense Science Board and the Navy, among others, argued for a rethinking of the principles of defense personnel management. In particular, the Naval Personnel Task Force 2000 contended that DoD's current static and centralized approach to human resource management would hinder its ability to capitalize on future opportunities and recommended allowing different skill groups to be managed differently. To prosper in an increasingly complex domestic and global environment, the military would have to be less uniform and more specialized. Moreover, not only would service needs and officer prerogatives have to be accommodated, but the need for high levels of performance from the diverse organizations that used officers would have to be considered.

REQUIREMENTS FOR OFFICERS: HOW MANY? WHAT KIND?

Requirements establish the vital need for officers, which must be satisfied at any cost: "It implies that we know what we want and that there is no room for debate about alternative solutions or substitutions."[9] Moreover, the term also falsely implies precision—a feasible, affordable mix of active, reserve, and civilian personnel defined by rating and paygrade or by a combination of skills and experience that minimizes costs and avoids mismatches between the demand and supply of personnel.[10] In reality, the collection of positions authorized to be filled with trained personnel must be adjusted to achieve the best balance among the requirements of force changes, available inventory, accession and separation predictions, fiscal constraints, and manpower ceilings.[11] Authorizations change instantaneously on

---

[9]David S.C. Chu, Director, Program Analysis and Evaluation, presentation to CNA workshop, 1982.

[10]Kostiuk (1987).

[11]DMRR (1995).

paper; the inventory of people changes slowly over long periods. Resolving inventory shortfalls against authorizations is difficult because both sides of the equation change constantly. Determining demand is no easier than creating supply.

The requirements issue seems straightforward: What are the characteristics and contributions that different groups of people bring to the workplace, and how many people of the various types are needed—and where and how do we use them? The Navy, as have the other services, has been wrestling with these questions for more than 200 years.

The Navy's challenges with determining and managing manpower requirements have existed since its birth. Congress has historically maintained a vigilant oversight on how the Navy is manned. In 1908, the Navy's challenges included the need to increase overall numbers, ensure a steady and adequate flow of promotion, adjust distribution, establish the grades of admiral and vice admiral, and improve the quality of senior officers.

To address the overall size of the force, a student at the War College, Commander Roy C. Smith, introduced the idea of establishing a ratio of numbers of personnel to tons of shipping. Although it was impractical to provide an estimate that would work for all ships, it was considered appropriate in obtaining an average overall ratio. Only battleships and cruisers were used to determine the size of the force, and a ratio of 3 commissioned officers/70 enlisted personnel per 1,000 tons was the standard he initially proposed. This ratio was further refined to 5 officers/100 enlisted personnel per 2,000 tons. It was not until passage of the Line Personnel Act of 1916 that this recommendation was acted upon. The number of officers would be based on a ratio to enlisted personnel, and the number of enlisted personnel was based on tonnage. Once this idea of ratios was adopted, the numbers of officers could be determined as a whole system and adjusted based on the size of the fleet.

How would the ratios developed in the early 1900s apply to ships of the line today? Table 2.1 exemplifies how the use of the 1916 manning standard (5 officers/100 enlisted personnel per 2,000 tons) would relate to ships of the line today.

Table 2.1

Early 20th-Century Manning Standards

Class ship	Tonnage (full load) Officer manning Enlisted manning	1908 manning ratio (5 officers/100 enlisted personnel per 2,000 tons)
CG-47	9,600	
	24	24
	340	480
DDG-51	8,300	
	23	21
	300	415
DD-963	9,100	
	30	23
	352	455
FFG-7	4,100	
	13	10
	287	205

NOTE: Tonnage data are from the United States Navy Fact File.

With the exception of the *Spruance*-class destroyer (DD-963), the ratio of officer manning to tonnage developed in the early 1900s compares closely to the actual officer manning ratios for the ships of the line of today.

While there appears to be a correlation with tonnage, the Navy has apparently moved away from "officers by the pound" and uses more sophisticated methods to determine needs. For example, in 1973, the Navy stated that force manpower for general purpose forces is derived on the basis of workload requirements for specific ship and aircraft types, which are then reflected in ship and squadron manning documents. The total requirement is also influenced by the need to provide shore billets for certain categories of personnel whose skill specialties are not required ashore in sufficient numbers to allow equitable sea/shore rotation patterns. A 1982 conference described the process as follows:

> Industrial engineers disaggregate each individual activity and then each required mission into tasks that must be performed as part of that mission. Once these tasks are identified, the time needed for each is measured by survey teams in a large sample of activities.

This process provides statistical confidence in the measure. The time needed per task is multiplied by the number of tasks per period. The result is the number of man-hours required per activity. Conversion from man-hours to manpower requirements is based on the length of the work-week. Because the work-week is shorter on shore than aboard ship, a given amount of work requires more manpower at a shore activity; on the other hand, tasks often differ between the two environments.[12]

However, criticism of methods used to determine officer (and enlisted) requirements continue. In its assessment of the 1988 Defense Officer Requirements Study (GAO, 1988), the General Accounting Office (GAO) reviewed its prior work on officer requirements. In particular, it concluded that none of the ground officer positions (support and administrative positions, such as flight surgeons, legal, maintenance, intelligence, and training) in squadron manpower documents was based on measured workload but was established largely on corporate management judgment. The GAO also expressed concerns about the credibility of the process for determining manpower needs for the shore establishment. During the mid-1980s, the Navy debated the merits of centralized and decentralized approaches to requirements with individuals and committees recommending alternatives. In 1988, the Secretary of the Navy chose a decentralized shore manpower program for both military and civilian personnel. The GAO was clear on its views:

> A manpower requirements determination system is essentially a control system. It helps ensure that the service has the number and kinds of positions it needs to carry out its mission while being mindful of the cost of additional manpower. We believe that the alternate proposal does not adequately address this control issue. Delegating the authority for manpower determination down to the user of that manpower while maintaining only a small central review function creates a lack of independence that impairs the credibility of statements of manpower requirements.[13]

The 1988 OSD study of defense officer requirements categorized causes for changes in officer requirements as follows:

---

[12]Blanco (1982).

[13]GAO (1988).

- **Force structure**—increases or decreases to the force structure and directly attributable support tail.

- **Structure/doctrinal change**—modifications to unit configuration or doctrine, causing unit adjustments.

- **Wartime shortages**—increases to address valid shortages.

- **Emerging technologies**—changes derived from evolving scientific and technical advances.

- **Changed functional requirements**—adjustments based on changed workload or methods of operation.

- **Joint/defense activities**—changes that directly support joint activities (e.g., activation/deactivation of commands/activities).

- **Training/transients**—changes to individual accounts as processes change.

- **Other**—includes classified programs.

Guidance for manpower is contained in DoD Directive 1100.4, which has been extant since August 20, 1954. The following three sections appear relevant:

> In areas which require military personnel only, manpower requirements shall be based upon applicable manning documents, with authorized strengths held to a minimum consistent with assigned tasks and missions. Civilian requirements will be determined on the basis of planning and workload factors with strengths maintained at the minimum necessary to accomplish the required tasks. In areas which require both military and civilian personnel, manpower requirements shall be determined as a total.

> The highest practicable proportion of Operating Forces to total forces will be maintained. Within the Operating Forces emphasis will be placed on reducing support type positions.

> Civilian personnel will be used in positions which do not require military incumbents for reasons of law, training, security, discipline, rotation, or combat readiness, which do not require a military background for successful performance of the duties involved, and which do not entail unusual hours not normally associated or compatible with civilian employment.

OSD (the Under Secretary of Defense for Personnel and Readiness) is responsible for reviewing and evaluating service manpower plans and programs. Annually, the services report programmed requirements, authorizations, and inventory that is published in the *Defense Manpower Requirements Report* (DMRR). The department's policy is to maintain as small an active peacetime force as national security policy, military strategy, and overseas commitments permit: "Department policy is to employ civilian employees and contractors wherever possible to free our military forces to perform military-specific functions. . . ."[14]

SUMMARY

Management of naval officers has changed over the years, reflecting the environment, missions, technology, and organization. The changes have seldom been easy and without controversy. The shift from equity to efficiency was debated for decades, if not an entire century. The emergence of service needs as a counter to individual officer prerogatives took nearly 100 years, and it has been another 70 years for the needs of organizations that use officers to be directly considered. There have been wide swings between flexible and structured management practices and between uniform and selective application of those practices. The most recent major legislation in 1980 (DOPMA) took the structured and uniform route. At the turn of the century, numerous studies suggest that flexibility and selective application might be the greater need to meet the emerging requirements for officers.

---

[14]DMRR (1995).

Chapter Three

OFFICER INVENTORY AND REQUIREMENTS: ANALYSIS OF HISTORICAL DATA

This chapter provides both a long- and near-term perspective on officer inventory and requirements. The long-term perspective takes at least a 50-year view of trends and factors that have shaped the inventory of naval officers. The report provides a historical analysis of officer requirements along several dimensions, including size, grade, experience, occupation, and the division between "tooth" and "tail." This analysis provides the data over time, compares the Navy with the other services, compares officers and enlisted personnel on some dimensions, and outlines several ratios for benchmark comparisons. The near-term perspective takes a 15-year look at both requirements for naval officers and the inventory available to meet requirements and serves as a baseline to estimate future inventory and requirements.

NAVAL OFFICERS, 1801–2001

Size of the Naval Officer Corps and Officer/Enlisted Composition

Figure 3.1 displays naval officer strength over the past 200 years. On the eve of the U.S. entry into World War II, there were roughly 12,000 naval officers, about half as many as were in service in 1918, the peak World War I year. During the entire 19th century, the number of naval officers exceeded 2,000 only during the Civil War. The number of officers began to grow in the early 20th century as the number and size of ships grew. (Beginning in 1916, and as described above, the number of officers was computed as a ratio of officers to enlisted personnel, the latter of which was based on the tonnage of a ship.)

During World War II, naval officer strength approached 350,000, with a total officer strength of about 1.1 million. Since then, naval officer strength has varied between 53,000 and 80,000.

The swings up and down were significant but are not of the magnitude of those that affect the Army, nor do they represent as significant a long-term trend downward as in the Air Force. Nor has the Navy been as stable as the Marine Corps officer force over time. In some respects, the Navy has had the best blend of size buildups and drawdowns, productivity and capability improvements, and stability of all the services.

Figure 3.2 highlights size differences for the second half of the 20th century for the officer corps in each service with respect to its present size.

The Army has always been the most affected by the cycle of buildup and drawdown. During both the Korean and Vietnam wars, the Army officer corps was nearly twice as large as it is today. After those two actions, it dropped to below 150 percent of its present size. The history of the Air Force officer corps has instead focused on missions, organization, and technology. In particular, during the Korean War era, the Air Force had more than 50,000 pilots compared with about 12,000 today. After the peak Vietnam years, the Air Force dropped from twice its present size to about 150 percent of its present size in the 1980s and then dropped the rest of the way in the 1990s. Much of the consistency in the Air Force evolution to its present size has to do with the constantly increasing capability in a nearly constantly decreasing force. A former Air Force chief of staff captured this productivity effect by ruminating how the Air Force has shifted from discussing how many sorties per target to how many targets per sortie.

The Marine Corps history tends to be one of constancy. While ups and downs in Korea and Vietnam did occur, they were not of the magnitude of those of the Army, and the Marine Corps has never been as large as 150 percent of its present size. The peak of the Marine Corps officer size compared with the present is about the same as the valley of the Army officer size, also compared with the present. The naval officer corps has seldom been 150 percent of its present size. The Navy has been up and down for national security needs, capability and productivity improvements, and presence and

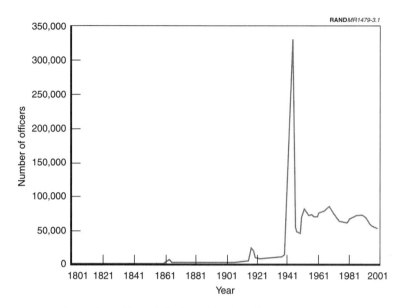

Figure 3.1—Size of the Naval Officer Corps, 1801–2001

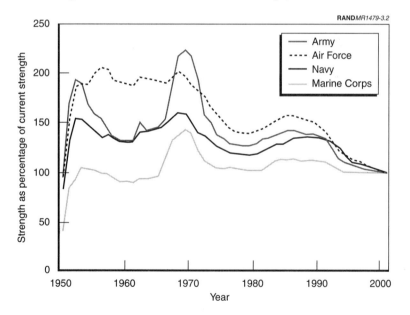

Figure 3.2—Service Strength as a Percentage of 2000 Strength, 1950–2001

constancy. Moreover, the Navy began the most recent drawdown later than the Army and Air Force, and therefore a more precipitous decline has occurred in the most recent years.

Over the long term, the naval officer strength has been more stable than either the Army or the Air Force, although if one focuses only on the last five years, the drop in size seems large and sudden.

In terms of an absolute comparison, Figure 3.3 contrasts the officer corps for each service over the second half of the 20th century.

The ratio between the enlisted and officer force also varies over time. Figure 3.4 presents the enlisted-to-officer ratio for the Navy from 1801 to 2001. It is striking that for long periods of both the 19th and 20th centuries, the ratio fluctuated between 6 and 10 enlisted sailors to each officer. A long aberration occurred from the time of the Spanish-American War through the pre–World War II period.

The "standing" active military began after the Spanish-American War and continued into the World War I era. However, officer strength did not increase as much as enlisted during this period, which accounts for the high enlisted-to-officer ratio for the first 20 years of the 20th century; it was about 20 to 1. Before World War I, brawn still mattered most. Coal-fired ships and legacy technology proportionally required more enlisted personnel.

The data show a significant shift from enlisted to officer manpower since World War I even as the Navy stayed at a total strength above 90,000 personnel. The introduction of the airplane, the modern steamship, the radio, and other new technologies shift work toward more use of brain than brawn. New technologies tend to be officer-heavy when first introduced because they are initially complex and require doctrinal and organizational change. Technological innovations also initially require a larger, officer-rich support tail to provide service and supply. Moreover, beginning in World War II and continuing to the present, the need to coordinate, integrate, and sustain naval forces numbering in the hundreds of thousands and not tens of thousands led to a substitution of officers for enlisted personnel to staff increasingly larger and more hierarchical organizations as well as the simple addition of more officers. Since World War II, there has been a continued downward trend with less-frequent spikes in the

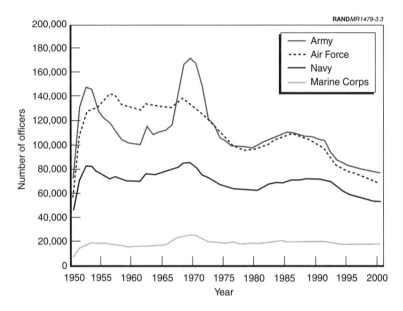

Figure 3.3—Officer Strength in Each Service, 1950–2001

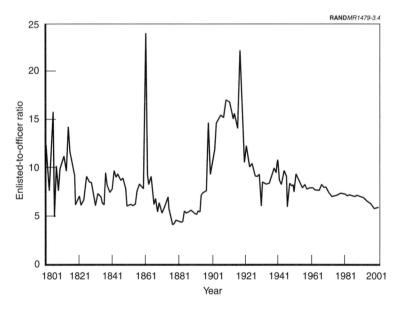

Figure 3.4—Navy Enlisted-to-Officer Ratio, 1801–2001

ratio (in times of conflict, the ratio tends to increase as more enlisted personnel are quickly added proportionally), as officers have come to represent a larger proportion of a large active military.

These ratios have trended downward in all services even as differences among services remained relatively constant as shown in Figure 3.5. The current ratio of enlisted to officer varies from around 9 to 1 in the Marine Corps, to 6 to 1 in the Navy, 5 to 1 in the Army, and 4 to 1 in the Air Force. Many of the differences by service can be accounted for by occupational composition. For example, the Air Force has a high proportion of pilots who are officers and a high proportion of technical personnel who are officers and thus a high officer content compared with enlisted. The Marine Corps has far fewer technical officer personnel proportionally compared with the other services and thus a higher enlisted-to-officer ratio; much of the Marine Corps support is supplied by the Navy. The Army has a somewhat higher percentage of officers in service and supply occupations than the Navy. Whether a more pronounced shift of technical, administrative, and service and supply to the enlisted force should occur in the future continues to be an open question.

This downward trend cannot continue forever. Looking forward, it is fair, for reasons to be outlined later, to assume that the enlisted force will begin to increase relative to the officer force but for both forces to be more highly experienced and graded.

GRADE STRUCTURE OF THE NAVAL OFFICER CORPS

The number of grades in the force has been reasonably stable: 10 commissioned officers[1] and 5 warrant officers. Grades O-9 and O-10 were added in 1958 and W-5 was added in 1993. The Navy has seldom used W-5 and uses W-1 infrequently. Grade O-7 has been used since 1971. The present quantified grade structure for the Navy appears in Figure 3.6.

---

[1]Grade O-11 existed through December 1965.

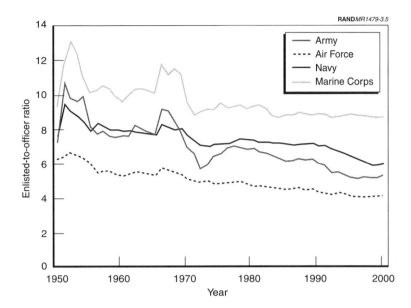

Figure 3.5—Enlisted-to-Officer Ratio in All Services, 1950–2001

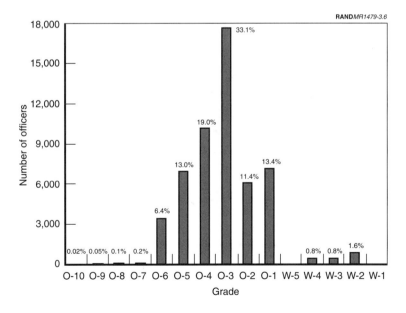

Figure 3.6—Officer Composition by Grade, 2001

Since 1958, within each respective grade structure (enlisted, commissioned, warrant) for each service, distributions have changed by becoming generally more senior as shown in Figures 3.7–3.9. Service differences exist, but for each service their present average grade is higher than in earlier eras. The growth is most consistent in the enlisted force where it ranges between 12 and 16 percent. The differences among services can be accounted for by career paths and retention. The Air Force has by far greater retention and greater demand for experienced personnel. The Marine Corps strives for a more junior force.

For commissioned officers, grade growth since the late 1970s is about 3 percent in the Army, 6 percent in both the Air Force and Navy, and 15 percent in the Marine Corps. Cycles are evident in both the enlisted and particularly in the commissioned officer forces as cohorts of different entry sizes work their way through the system over time and confront promotion phase points. (The controlled grade tables for O-4 to O-6 have increased several times since 1980.)

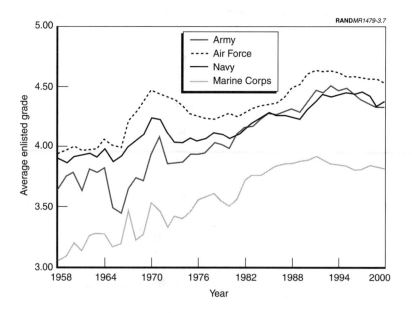

Figure 3.7—Average Enlisted Grade, 1958–2000

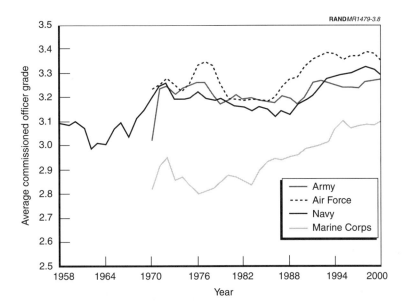

Figure 3.8—Average Commissioned Officer Grade, 1958–2000

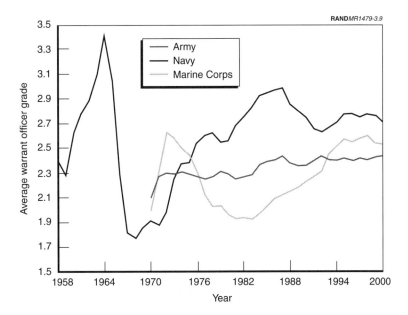

Figure 3.9—Average Warrant Officer Grade, 1958–2000

For warrant officers, the cycles are pronounced in the Navy and Marine Corps. There is more stability in the Army because of the larger numbers of warrant officers. Grade averages have increased, and the Marine Corps now has a higher grade average than the Army.

Differently sized entry cohorts, advancement and retention patterns, and grade controls have trend and cyclical effects in a closed system that differ by service and category of the workforce. These dynamic effects also reflect higher levels of responsibility and higher compensation.

Congress oversees the grade content of the O-1 to O-6 commissioned officer force through the use of authorized strengths for lieutenant commander, commander, and captain. These authorizations for each grade are contained in Title 10 U.S. Code and are based on a "sliding scale" in that more senior officers are allowed as the total number of commissioned officers becomes smaller. A portrayal of the aggregate allowed strengths for O-4 to O-6 is shown in Figure 3.10. The original DOPMA-controlled grade table was modified permanently in FY 1997 to reflect lower total commissioned officer strengths than were envisioned in 1981 and to raise the allowed strengths by about 2 percent at every strength level. Moreover, Congress allowed for a temporary number of O-4, O-5, and O-6 officers for FY 1996 and FY 1997. The percentages allowed (based on the specific number of officers authorized) for those two years were about 45 percent.

For computing the number of officers allowed, general and flag officers, warrant officers, medical officers, and dental officers are excluded from both numerator and denominator. The FY 2000 commissioned officer strength excluding these categories is about 46,400 officers, and therefore about 40.8 percent of officer strength is allowed in grades O-4 to O-6. The comparable number in 1988 would have been 63,800 total officers and 34.7 percent of officer strength, reflecting a higher total officer strength and a lower grade table.

Why are the numbers higher? A House committee in its report accompanying the authorization recognized that there had been an increase in the requirements for officers in grades O-4, O-5, and O-6 since 1980 that had limited the ability of the services to comply with promotion timing and opportunity rates. The Senate Armed Services

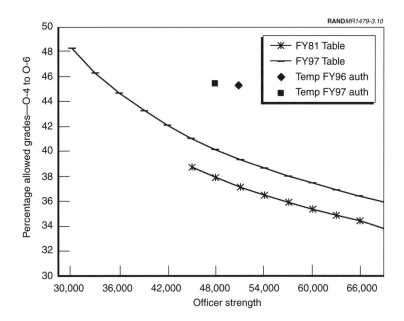

RAND*MR1479-3.10*

Figure 3.10—Controlled Grade Table, Navy

Committee in its report was more explicit. The committee stated that the change should assist the services in meeting the increased field-grade requirements resulting from the continued implementation of Goldwater-Nichols; permit all services to cease or greatly reduce the practice of frocking to circumvent the statutory grade ceilings; reduce promotion flow points; and allow the services to realign the number of officers selected for promotion in a particular year with the number of officers that can be expected to be promoted. (While increased requirements were mentioned, it is clear from both committee reports that DOPMA promotion practices are meant to supply officers at a specified rate over time.) Moreover, the Senate concluded with the following:

> The committee also notes that, historically, many specialty corps officers in the military services, such as the Nurse Corps, may not have had sufficient field grade authorizations to meet requirements in those specialties. The committee expects that the military services having specialty corps will allocate the permanent grade relief provided in this provision among line and specialty corps in an equitable, requirement-based manner. The committee believes

that a result of such an allocation will be more consistent promotion opportunities among line and specialty corps officers.[2]

The effect of this language will become apparent in the next section where we match authorizations and inventories over time.

Overall grade trends for all Navy commissioned officers are shown in Figure 3.11. The trends are similar but at a lower level if doctors and dentists are excluded.

The increase in the O-1 to O-3 content, as seen in Figure 3.11 and shown in more detail in Figure 3.12, in the 1980s is attributable to several factors and is instructive in explaining how many forces shape an inventory of officers. We cannot attribute cause and effect to any of these, but all play a part. Usually one can see a clear pattern of lagged grade growth depending on promotion timing—for example, O-2s grow two years after O-1s grow. That pattern is observable in Figure 3.12 up until the early 1980s. During the Reagan administrations, O-3 growth appears unrelated to more junior officer change in earlier years. Part of the increase is attributable to retention growth: Those who are already O-3s are staying longer.

Higher retention for O-3s during the Reagan buildup may be related to opportunities (and a steady paycheck) in the Navy as compared with opportunities for civilian employment. During this time there were more ships, more people, more command billets to advance to, and perhaps a steadier personnel rotation plan that may also account for a greater propensity to stay. In addition, 1992 was a high-water mark for unemployment rates. From 1992 to the present, there has been a steady decline in unemployment and greater civilian opportunities. Higher retention of O-3s in the 1980s could have been a reflection of decreased opportunities for employment in the private sector and relative changes in military/civilian compensation as a result of the approximately 25-percent increases in basic pay in the early 1980s. Another factor that may account for the growth of O-3s is the change in the promotion opportunity and time-in-service or promotion to O-4 (see Table 3.1). Opportunity decreases and

[2]104th Congress, Second Session, *National Defense Authorization Act for Fiscal Year 1997*, United States Senate, Report 104-267, May 13, 1996.

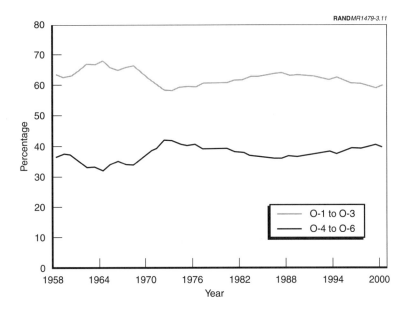

Figure 3.11—Navy Grade Trends, 1958–2001

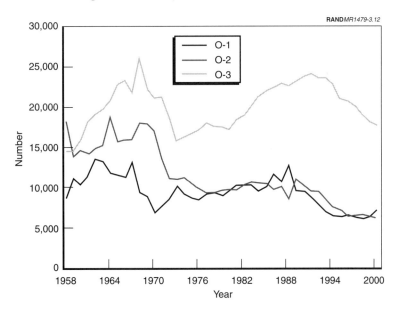

Figure 3.12—Navy O-1 to O-3 Trends, 1958–2001

time-in-service at promotion increases to O-4 even though both
continue to significantly exceed the DOPMA goals for each.[3] For
example, the promotion opportunity to O-4 reached a peak of 97
percent in 1979, when the promotion point was nine years and three
months in service. By 1990, the promotion opportunity was down to
85.7 percent, and the promotion point extended to ten years and five
months in service. Many dynamics shape the inventory at any given
time.

Fluctuation in the grade content of the officer corps is muted compared with that of the 19th century. Figure 3.13 compares three different time periods. Until 1910, different laws affected the Army and
the Navy, or no laws pertained at all. There was a seniority promotion system (all had to be promoted; you just had to wait your turn)
and after 1916 some forced attrition was used. Depending on
buildups and drawdowns and longevity in the senior ranks, the grade
content of O-4 to O-6 ranged from as high as 70 percent to as low as
10 percent. After grade controls were implemented following World
War II, there was less variation in the O-4 to O-6 grade content
because fully qualified officers were required to leave after failing
promotion twice. The seniority system continued with most remaining officers promoted. In the DOPMA era, O-4 to O-6 content has
varied within 5 percentage points within a seniority promotion system with forced attrition.

Occupations

Each service has a distinct occupational or skill mix. The officer distribution for each service is shown in Figure 3.14 and the enlisted
distribution appears in Figure 3.15.[4]

---

[3]The DOPMA promotion goals are 80 percent to O-4, 70 percent to O-5, and 50 percent to O-6.

[4]For these portrayals, the DoD Occupational Coding System is aggregated as follows.
Officer: General Military (Tactical Operations Officers), Technical (Intelligence, Engi-
neering/Maintenance, Scientist/Professionals, Health Care), Administrative
(Administrators), and Service and Supply (Supply/Procurement). Enlisted: General
Military (Infantry/Seamanship), Technical (Electronic Repair, Other Tech/Allied,
Communications/Intelligence, Health Care), Administrative (Functional Support/
Administrative), Service and Supply (Service and Supply Handlers), and Craftsmen
(Craftsmen, Electric/Mechanical Repair).

Table 3.1

Navy Promotion Opportunities (Percentage) and Promotion Points (Years-Months)

Fiscal Year	Grade									
	O-6		O-5		O-4		O-3		O-2	
	%	PP	%	PP	%	PP	%	PP	%	PP
1999	60.0	21-4	75.0	15-2	80.0	9-11	99.3	4-0	FQ	2-0
1998	60.0	21-4	75.0	15-2	80.0	10-1	99.0	4-0	FQ	2-0
1997	59.9	21-2	70.0	15-8	70.0	10-4	98.8	4-0	FQ	2-0
1996	52.9	21-2	70.8	15-8	76.8	9-8	99.6	4-0	FQ	2-0
1995	53.1	21-1	70.7	15-6	76.5	9-7	99.4	4-0	FQ	2-0
1994	53.0	21-0	70.8	15-5	76.8	10-5	99.6	4-0	FQ	2-0
1993	54.2	21-0	68.0	15-6	75.7	10-4	95.7	4-0	FQ	2-0
1992	55.3	21-11	70.3	16-0	76.4	10-8	95.5	4-0	FQ	2-0
1991	55.1	22-1	72.5	16-4	82.7	10-8	97.3	4-0	FQ	2-0
1990	55.6	22-3	72.0	16-6	85.7	10-5	97.0	4-0	FQ	2-0
1989	55.4	22-5	71.8	15-11	82.7	9-10	96.0	4-0	FQ	2-0
1988	56.0	21-1	72.0	15-2	82.0	9-10	94.9	4-3	FQ	2-0
1987	56.6	21-0	73.5	15-1	83.1	9-8	94.7	4-0	FQ	2-0
1986	57.0	20-11	74.0	15-6	83.0	9-6	96.0	4-0	FQ	2-0
1985	57.6	21-0	76.3	15-3	85.8	9-5	95.0	4-0	FQ	2-0
1984	60.0	21-3	75.0	15-1	84.0	9-4	98.8	4-0	FQ	2-0
1983	61.0	21-5	80.0	14-9	85.0	9-2	98.3	4-0	FQ	2-0

Table 3.1—continued

Fiscal Year	O-6		O-5		O-4		O-3		O-2	
	%	PP	%	PP	%	PP	%	PP	%	PP
1982	70.0	21-6	82.0	14-9	90.0	9-2	97.1	4-0	FQ	2-0
1981	70.0	21-5	85.0	14-8	95.0	9-0	95.0	4-0	FQ	2-0
1980	62.5	21-9	80.0	14-9	90.0	9-3	95.0	4-0	FQ	2-0
1979	60.0	21-9	70.0	14-10	97.0	9-3	95.0	4-0	FQ	2-0
1978	60.0	21-6	70.0	14-5	85.0	9-0	95.0	4-0	FQ	2-0
1977	60.0	20-10	70.0	14-9	80.0	9-3	95.0	4-0	FQ	2-0
1976	60.0	21-0	70.0	15-2	75.0	9-0	95.0	4-0	FQ	2-0
1975	60.0	21-0	70.0	15-9	75.0	8-11	95.0	4-0	FQ	2-0
1974	60.0	20-9	70.0	15-0	75.0	8-9	95.0	4-0	FQ	2-0
1973	60.0	20-6	70.0	15-0	85.0	8-6	NA	NA	FQ	NA
1972	60.0	20-6	75.0	14-6	90.0	8-0	NA	NA	FQ	NA

NOTE: The above statistics represent the average promotion opportunity (%) and promotion points (PP) of all competitive categories within a service. Promotion opportunity is computed by totaling all officers selected from in (IPZ), above (APZ), and below (BPZ) zone and dividing by the total number of officers considered in-zone (IPZ + APZ + BPZ) / IPZ. Promotion points are computed by the number of years and months of active commissioned service plus entry credit when officers are promoted to a particular grade. FQ denotes that all who were fully qualified were promoted.

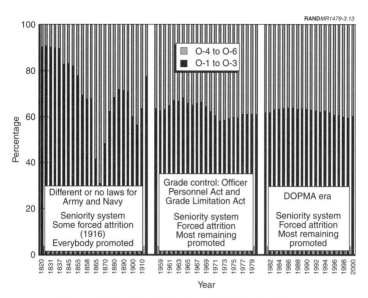

Figure 3.13—Grade Content for Selected Years

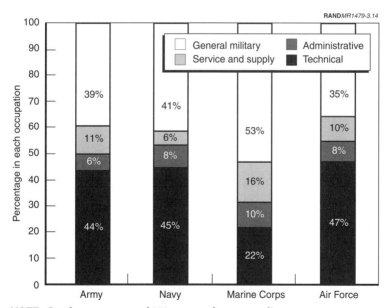

NOTE: Graphs may not equal 100 percent due to rounding.

Figure 3.14—Officer Occupational Distribution, 2001

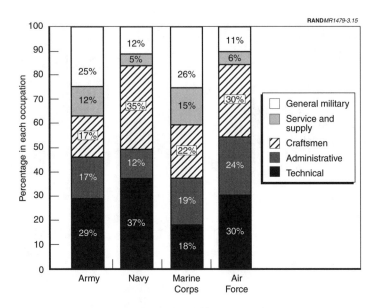

NOTE: Graphs may not equal 100 percent due to rounding.

Figure 3.15—Enlisted Occupational Distribution, 2001

The Marine Corps has the highest percentage of its officer force in general military occupations. The Air Force has the most technical personnel proportionally. The Navy is second in both categories. The service and supply/administrative occupations range from 14 percent in the Navy to 26 percent in the Marine Corps.

The enlisted distribution has both the Marine Corps and Army at the highest proportions of general military. The Navy has the most technical personnel, while the Marine Corps has the least. Included in the Navy's technical category are health services personnel, many of whom provide that service to the Marine Corps. Craftsmen account for large proportions in the Navy and Air Force.

Figure 3.16 provides a side-by-side comparison of the officer and enlisted distribution for the Navy. The percentage of distributions differ (notably that there are no craftsmen among the officers). Officers are almost evenly split between technical and general military, while enlisted are almost split evenly between technical and craftsmen.

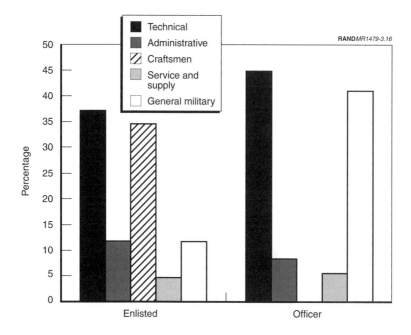

**Figure 3.16—Enlisted and Officer Occupational
Distribution in the Navy, 2001**

This occupational distribution is far from static. Figure 3.17 shows how the enlisted distribution has changed since the World War I era for all services in the aggregate. Data are not readily available for officer occupations in the early years, but that period likely had changes similar to what has occurred more recently. The precipitous decline in jobs classified as general military is quite evident as is the equally marked increase in craftsmen and technical occupations.

The organization of work and the composition of the military force change with mission, organization, and technology. During the early years of the military, before World War I, there was little demand for occupational specialization. Most soldiers were riflemen, although a few others served in support activities. The Navy was the first to experience the effect of the Industrial Revolution. The shift from sails to steam was a far-reaching technological change. The Army lagged behind for several decades until its World War I mobilization,

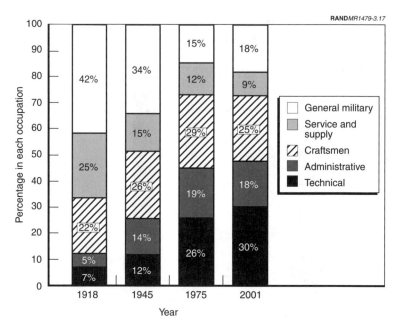

NOTE: Graphs may not equal 100 percent due to rounding.

Figure 3.17—Enlisted Occupational Distribution, 1918–2001

but the subsequent transformation was quite dramatic. For the first time, the combat soldier was in a numerical minority.

Following World War II, several factors dramatically changed the occupational requirements of the services. Among them were the acceleration of weapons and military technology to include nuclear capability, application of electronics to communications and logistics, and the emergence of missiles and air defense. Organizational structures changed to take advantage of the new armaments and processes. Another noticeable shift began in the occupational distribution away from infantry, artillery, and seaman skills and toward technical fields. Having grown large by 1975, technical workers by 1984 constituted the largest of the five separate groupings as they do today.[5] As of 2001, 18 percent of the enlisted force were in a general

---

[5]Another major milestone in workforce composition occurred in 1985. For the first time, more selective reservists and DoD civilian employees than active military personnel were in the defense workforce.

military specialty, 34 percent were blue-collar workers (service and supply workers and craftsmen), and 48 percent were white-collar workers (administrative and technical workers). The percentage of service and supply, craftsmen, and administrative has begun to decrease.

Experience

Figure 3.18 shows the present experience distribution for each service with officer and enlisted personnel aggregated together. The Marine Corps is the most junior, and the Air Force has the most senior personnel.

Figure 3.19 shows how the naval officer experience has changed over time. Certain patterns are noticeable, particularly the experience

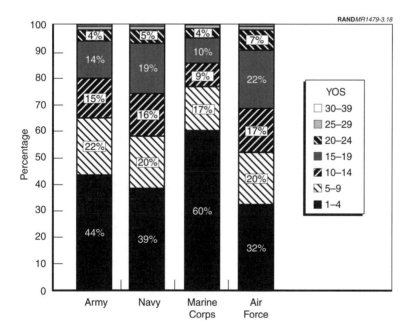

NOTE: Graphs may not equal 100 percent due to rounding.

Figure 3.18—Distribution of Years of Service, May 2001

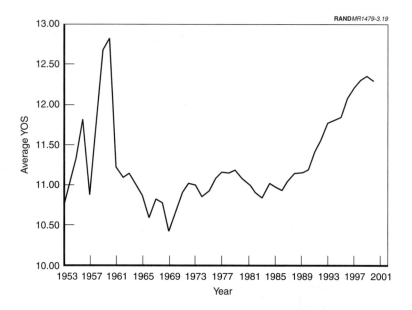

Figure 3.19—Naval Officer Experience, 1953–2000

legacy in the 1950s from the World War II and Korean War eras. During past buildups (e.g., for the Vietnam War), average experience went down, especially as junior officers entered for limited service. Moreover, in such periods, retention also decreased. With the advent of the All-Volunteer Force, and especially as a result of the Reagan era, officer experience has increased significantly.

However, it is not just changes in average experience that must be accommodated. Various periods of significant buildup and draw-down, and even relatively minor strength changes, cause tidal waves of experience surges in a static, cohort (year group)–based system. This is illustrated in Figure 3.20, which portrays the distribution of experience for naval officers in selected periods. For several of these periods, an "average" experience level is completely misleading. The force was junior and senior, not average. The 1957 force provides the most startling example, with large spikes at 1 and 11 years of experience.

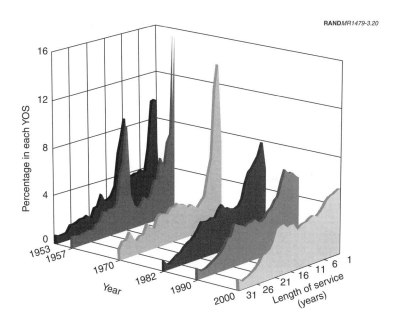

Figure 3.20—Naval Officer Experience, Selected Periods

Swings occur constantly, as Figure 3.21 shows. The figure highlights the tremendous peaks and valleys that occur in experience, with sharp spikes occurring in the early years of a cohort during buildups and those spikes continuing into the future. Behind the peaks in a closed system are the valleys. Being able to manage a constantly changing experience distribution across periods of time is one of the more difficult tasks that a personnel management system must accomplish.

OTHER BENCHMARKS

We have been asked to provide several ratios that might be used as benchmarks or that highlight trends. Several are proffered here. The first is to contrast use of Department of the Navy civilians[6] and

---

[6]The historical data series used aggregates Navy and Marine Corps civilian employees into a Department of the Navy number.

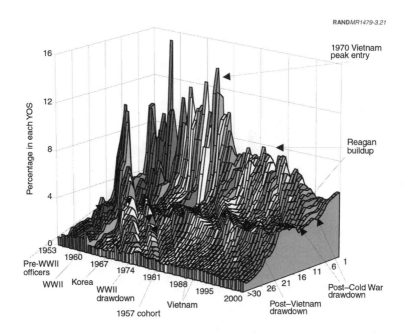

RAND*MR1479-3.21*

Figure 3.21—Naval Officer Experience Distribution, 1953–2000

selected reservists with the use of naval officers. Figure 3.22 shows a ratio of each to officers. The ratio of civilians per officer has gone down, which means that proportionally over time and in particular for the last 10 years, more manpower is being provided by naval officers. The change in the ratio of selected reservists to officers is even more stark, falling from near 6 to 1 in the early 1970s to less than 2 to 1 currently.

Another interesting contrast is found in the examination of the same trends for the other services. Figure 3.23 provides the comparison, which shows the ratios trending in the opposite direction. Use of civilians compared with officers has trended down for all in the last five years. In general, use of civilians and reservists reduces the need for uniformed manpower, all other things being equal.

We also examined the use of capital goods and services as a ratio to each naval officer and compared such use with the other services.

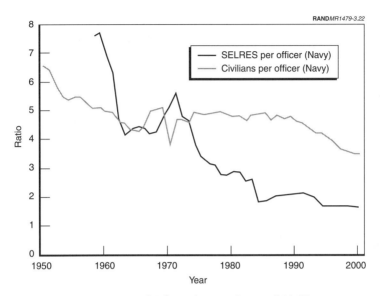

**Figure 3.22—Ratio of Selected Reservists and Civilians to
Naval Officers, 1950–2001**

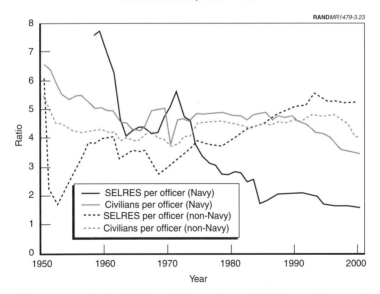

**Figure 3.23—Ratio of Selected Reservists and Civilians, Navy and
Non-Navy, to Officers, 1950–2001**

Figure 3.24 shows contract awards by procurement program in 1996 dollars for hard goods and services per naval officer. In a broad sense, capital (goods and technology) and contractor labor (services) have grown more rapidly than naval officers. Since the 1950s, there has been a threefold real increase in constant dollars per officer for hard goods; this, all other things being equal, reduces the need for uniformed manpower as capital is being substituted for labor. Such investments are "lumpy" and, depending on the useful life of the capital goods, do not need to be made every year. During the Reagan years, significant capital investments were made. With the "procurement holiday" of the 1990s, the Navy is currently investing the same amount per officer in aircraft, missile and space systems, ships, tank-automotive, weapons, ammunition, and electronics and communications equipment as was invested in most of the 1960s and 1970s. Services tend to be consumed each year and represent a substitution of one type of labor for another—in this case for Navy

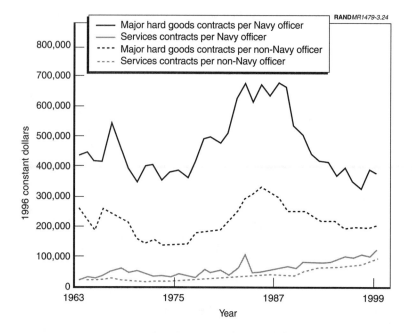

Figure 3.24—Capital and Services Leverage: Navy and
Non-Navy, 1963–2000

personnel; 1999 constant dollar expenditures on services per officer were more than four times larger than 1963 expenditures ($23,000 compared with about $95,000).   All other things being equal, increased spending on goods and services reduces the need for military personnel. The trends for the other services are the same, but the Navy makes a larger capital and services investment per officer compared with the other services.

Figure 3.25 compares the several workforces of the Navy. Over the last 40 years, officer, enlisted, and Department of the Navy civilian personnel have grown proportionally compared with those in the selected reserves.

Removing selected reservists from the workforce changes the portrait somewhat, as shown in Figure 3.26. Officers have increased significantly as a percentage of the workforce since 1958.

"TOOTH-TO-TAIL" ISSUES AND PATTERNS

"Tooth-to-tail" ratios are of interest to those trying to characterize the amount of warfighting ability ("tooth") afforded by the supporting "tail." There is no one definition for the concept of tooth to tail. Multiple ways exist to characterize units and personnel as either tooth or tail, and analysts and policymakers frequently seize on one or the other to make particular points. In 1973, DoD presented seven different views of combat-to-support ratios, and variations of these have since existed.   These views ranged from ones based on individual skills to those based on different aggregations of major defense programs. For the Navy, in 1973, the seven different views produced ratios (percentages of tooth) that ranged from 11 to 60 percent.

Currently at least five views appear prevalent in Navy, OSD, or other organization use for what amounts to a tooth-to-tail ratio:

1. **Defense Mission Categories.** This is the view used in such documents as the DMRR and in reports such as that on tooth-to-tail ratios recently prepared by the Business Executives for National Security. In this view, the operating forces are considered tooth while the eight categories of defense infrastructure are considered tail. For the active Navy (officer and enlisted) in FY 1999

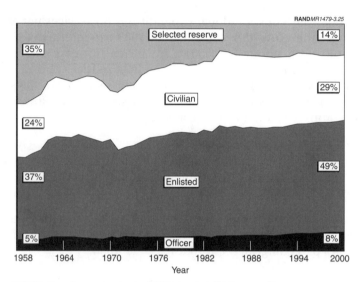

NOTE: Graphs may not equal 100 percent due to rounding.

**Figure 3.25—Proportion of Naval Officer, Enlisted, Civilian, and
Selected Reserve Personnel, 1958–2000**

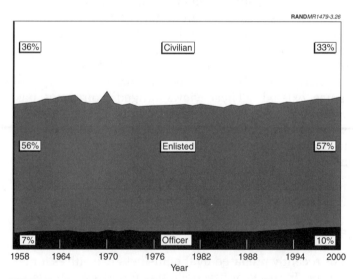

NOTE: Graphs may not equal 100 percent due to rounding.

**Figure 3.26—Proportion of Naval Officer, Enlisted, and
Civilian Personnel, 1958–2000**

(from the DMRR), the operating force structure had 191,700 of 373,000 people—or 51.3 percent of the total. In essence, by this definition, Supply Corps or Medical Corps officers in operating units would be tooth and unrestricted line officers in training or base operations would be tail. The emphasis is on use of officers, not on their individual attributes. Moreover, for particular purposes, one could combine defense mission categories (and the underlying program element codes) in various ways that could lead to different percentages of tooth or tail.[7]

2. **DoD Occupational Codes.** DoD has an occupational classification system that relates all service occupations (designators, Military Occupational Specialty, etc.) within a common hierarchy. This classification scheme can be used in a myriad of ways depending on the purpose of the study.[8] This is the scheme that the Congressional Budget Office (CBO) used as the basis for its 1999 report. In that report, CBO considered general officers, tactical occupations, engineering occupations, and intelligence occupations to be combat and all others to be support. By this definition, 53.5 percent of naval officers were considered combat or tooth. However, one could vary this percentage by removing engineers or intelligence officers from the tooth side of the calculation. Moreover, the emphasis in this calculation is on officer attributes (not use).

3. **Unrestricted Line as a Percentage of Officers.** This calculation is frequently portrayed within the Navy personnel community and can be built from either authorization or inventory data—50.8

---

[7]OPNAV Instruction No. 100.16J (Department of the Navy [Office of the Chief of Naval Operations], 1998) prescribes the use of the terms combat manpower and support manpower. *Combat manpower* is associated with ships and aircraft squadrons, while *support manpower* is associated with shore activities. It states: "These terms are defined in terms of the placement of individual units and associated manpower within official Defense Mission Codes (DMCs) as reflected in the FYDP [Future Years Defense Program]. Combat manpower is all manpower associated with units included in the Strategic Forces and General Purpose Forces DMCs. Support manpower is all manpower associated with units included in other categories." The historical data we present beginning with Figure 3.27 are consistent with this definition. We recognize that, in practice, many Navy officers disregard this conception and associate unrestricted line, even if in shore activities, with combat or "tooth."

[8]We used DoD occupational codes earlier to describe enlisted and officer aggregate occupations.

percent for the former and 50.3 percent for the latter. It measures attributes of officers, not their use. The difference between this and the prior CBO study is most likely its inclusion of engineering and intelligence officers as part of combat.

4. **Sea Duty (Afloat) Officers as a Percentage of Officers.** This frequently used calculation can be derived from multiple sources, all using slightly different definitions of at sea or afloat. This definition focuses on a form of use of officers (location), not their attributes, but it is a different calculation of use from the first view outlined above.

5. **Officers in Unit Accounts vs. Officers in Individuals Accounts.** Individuals accounts are used for officers who are in training, who are transients, who are patients, or who are in a status where they cannot be attributed to units or activities. Typically, the individuals account for naval officers is about 18 percent of total officer end strength.

In sum, over the years a number of methods have been used to calculate combat-to-support or tooth-to-tail ratios that can lead to wide swings in results. Using any of them is arguable—especially if the inference is good or bad—as these comparisons are analytically clouded and loaded with pejorative interpretations. When used, they should at least be consistent over time, portray the basis for calculating them, and inform users of the alternative methods of calculating the ratios.

Presented below are a series of figures that use a ratio of officers in strategic and operating forces to all officers. This is the first definition presented above, which the Navy formally uses. We must caution, however, that the specific program element codes that make up the defense mission categories change from time to time. Figure 3.27 shows the ratio by grade from 1985 to the present. The highest percentage is grade O-2, where nearly 70 percent of officers are in the Strategic and General Purpose Forces programs. Grades O-3 and O-4 are at the Navy average of 44 percent. The more senior grades of O-5 and O-6 have fewer proportionately in the operating forces, with O-5 at 38 percent and O-6 at 28 percent. Grade O-1 is an aberration; many of the most junior officers are accounted for in the training account, not in the operational accounts.

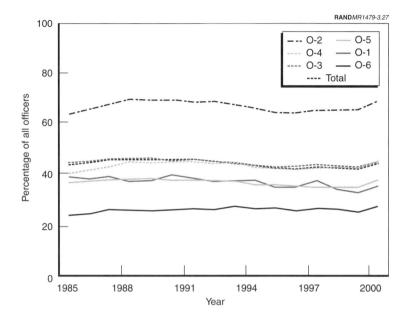

NOTE: Numerator is the number of officers in Strategic and General Purpose
Forces programs.

**Figure 3.27—Percentage of Naval Officers by Grade in
Strategic and General Forces Programs**

Figure 3.28 presents the same data broken out by community. The
CWO and LDO[9] communities have the highest percentage in the

---

[9]The Navy has the limited duty officer (LDO) and chief warrant officer (CWO) programs that provide commissioning opportunities to senior enlisted personnel. Chief
petty officers (E-7 through E-9) and E-6 personnel who are eligible to go before the E-7
selection board may apply for the LDO or CWO program. A bachelor's degree is not
required; however, it is strongly desirable for selection.

LDOs are technically oriented officers who perform duties in specific occupational
fields and require strong managerial skills. LDOs serve in a wide variety of specialties
to include deck (surface ships and submarines), operations, engineering/repair, ordnance, electronics, communications, and aviation deck and operations.

CWOs are technical specialists who perform duties requiring extensive knowledge and
skills of a specific occupational field. CWOs may apply for the LDO program and may
accept appointment to lieutenant (junior grade O-2) or vice ensign (O-1). CWOs also

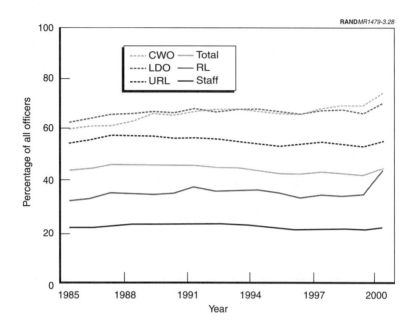

NOTE: Numerator is the number of officers in Strategic and General Purpose Forces programs.

Figure 3.28—Naval Officers by Community in Strategic and General Forces Programs

operating force mission areas at about 70 percent. Unrestricted line is next at 55 percent. Restricted line is at the community average of about 44 percent. Staff is at 21 percent. Presenting the data by mis-

---

serve in a wide variety of specialties to include boatswain (surface deck force), operations technician, engineering technician, engineering repair technician, and ordnance and electronic technicians.

Upon selection for the LDO or CWO program, candidates attend a five-week school. The LDO/CWO course, "Mustang [a person who came up through the ranks from enlisted to officer] University," is designed to enhance the candidate's professionalism, self-confidence, and ability to meet the challenges and increased demands of an officer.

LDOs and CWOs are well respected. They are looked up to by the troops as leaders who have been in their shoes and can more easily relate to their challenges as well as provide clear guidance and direction on how to perform their assignments. Line officers respect the experience, technical expertise, and problem-solving abilities that LDOs provide.

sion categories (uses of officers) highlights the fact that not all unrestricted line officers are "tooth" by this definition, nor are all staff "tail." Moreover, the CWO and LDO communities have by far the highest proportion of their numbers in Strategic and General Purpose Forces.

The next series of figures (3.29–3.32) present the data by community. While the levels of content vary across community as shown above, within each community the pattern is similar to the all-Navy grade pattern. In general, the more junior officers (with the exception of O-1 because of its presence in the training accounts) account for a higher percentage of content in Strategic and General Purpose Forces programs.

SUMMARY

Over its 200-year history, the Navy and its officer corps have been large and small, and presently there are fewer officers than at any time since immediately after World War II. For nearly 100 years, officers have routinely supplanted enlisted personnel within the Navy end strength, but there is some evidence that this practice may have reached a nadir. Following the Vietnam War expansion and its influx of junior officers, the naval officer corps has continued to increase in average experience and grade. The officer corps of today has about two more years of experience on average than it had in 1970. The Navy has proportionally fewer officers in service and supply and administrative occupations than any other service, including the Marine Corps. Technical occupations make up 45 percent of the officer corps. Compared with the other services, the Navy has proportionally fewer selected reservists and civilians as complements to the officer corps but uses more goods and services contract dollars. The proportion of officers in combat forces has been reasonably stable at about 44 percent for the last 15 years.

This data-based review of naval officer corps history should serve as a lens from which to view the future. Before we estimate the future demand and supply of officers (2000–2017), we review in the next chapter how well the Navy has done in managing the officer corps to meet its recent demand.

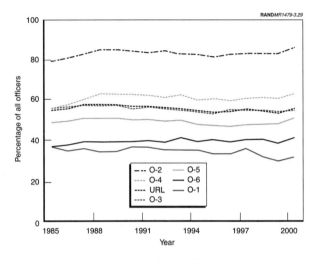

NOTE: Numerator is the number of officers in Strategic and General Purpose Forces programs.

Figure 3.29—Navy Unrestricted Line Officers in Strategic and General Forces Programs

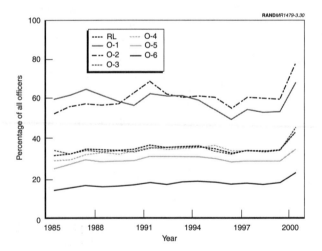

NOTE: Numerator is the number of officers in Strategic and General Purpose Forces programs.

Figure 3.30—Navy Restricted Line Officers in Strategic and General Forces Programs

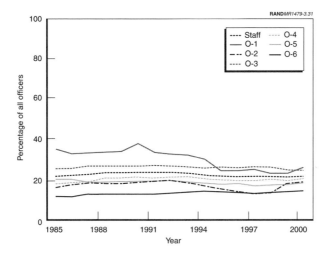

NOTE: Numerator is the number of officers in Strategic and General Purpose Forces programs.

Figure 3.31—Navy Staff Corps Officers in Strategic and General Forces Programs

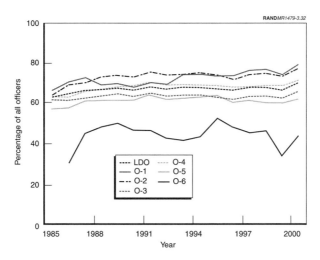

NOTE: Numerator is the number of officers in Strategic and General Purpose Forces programs.

Figure 3.32—Navy LDOs in Strategic and General Forces Programs

Chapter Four

GAP ANALYSIS:
DELTAS, DIFFERENCES, AND MISMATCHES

We define "gap" as any delta, difference, or mismatch of inventory to Billets Authorized (BA). The inventory of officers can differ from BA in several ways. Shortages or overages of officers might exist within a designator or there might be the correct number of officers, but the grade structure within the designator might be askew, resulting in too many or too few senior officers. We include all of these in our use of "gap" regardless of whether there is an excess or shortage of officers compared with BA.

ALLOCATION OF 1000 AND 1050 BILLETS

Before proceeding with a discussion of manning gaps, we believe it is important to establish how we analytically addressed Navy billets that are not directly associated with officers of a particular designator. Although most Navy billet descriptions identify the particular kind of officer that should fill the billet, there is considerably more leeway in determining which officers are assigned to 1000 and 1050 billets.[1] Nonetheless, filling these billets is part of the manpower burden placed on the communities eligible to fill 1000 and 1050 billets, and thus we have included 1000 and 1050 billets in the BA and have distributed them proportionately across the appropriate designators by grade. For example, in FY 2000, O-6 aviators constituted 36 percent of O-6 unrestricted line and special duty officer inventory. By our method, we then attribute 36 percent of O-6 1000 billets to

---

[1] 1000 billets can be filled either by any unrestricted line officer or any special duty officer; 1050 billets can only be filled by an unrestricted line–qualified warfighter.

O-6 aviators in FY 2000. These percentages change considerably by grade over fiscal years.[2]

DELTAS BETWEEN AUTHORIZATIONS AND INVENTORY

Most Navy officer communities evidence some degree of gap between authorizations and inventory. There are multiple explanations for, and patterns evident in, these mismatches. This analysis indicates some of these patterns and explanations, using selected communities.[3] We present an observation and then data that support it.

More Fluctuation Among the Most Junior Grades

One finding that emerges from analyzing these inventory-versus-authorization data is that very few universal patterns emerge from a preliminary analysis because each community differs. Thus, this section will illuminate some of those differences and explanations for varying patterns of systemic behavior. Figures 4.1–4.6 display the manpower history of surface warfare officers (SWOs; designators 111x and 116x), and Figures 4.7–4.12 show aviation officers (designators 130x, 131x, 132x, 137x, and 139x). It is apparent from these data that there is more fluctuation and variance in grades O-1 and O-2 than in the later grades[4]; the system can react more quickly to demands for additional personnel at the junior grades, but those adjustments are less easy to control because the retention behavior of junior officers can vary. The surface warfare and aviation communities show less variance among the senior grades, which suffer fewer gaps.

---

[2]In Harrell, Thie, et al. (2001) we note that the Navy does not assign officers proportionately to 1000 and 1050 billets outside the Navy. Rather, aviators are assigned to these billets at a disproportionately high rate. However, the authors suggest that, if all other assignment issues (such as excess inventory) are resolved, then assigning officers proportionately to 1000 and 1050 billets would be a more cost-efficient use of officers, given the greater expense of developing and retaining an aviator.

[3]Data regarding all Navy communities are available, upon request, from the authors.

[4]Calculations of the mean-adjusted standard deviation reveal substantially higher variance in O-1 and O-2 than in later grades. For the surface, submarine, aviation, Nurse Corps, and Supply Corps communities, average variation within O-1 to O-2 is 60 percent larger than variation within O-3 to O-6.

For example, Figure 4.1 shows a spike in inventory representing a large cohort entering the grade of O-1 at the beginning of the 1990s. After this cohort is promoted to O-2, the figure indicates a shortage of O-1s for a few years (compared with authorizations). However, Figures 4.2 and 4.3 show excess inventory compared with authorizations, especially as the large 1990 cohort is promoted to O-2 and then O-3. Figures 4.4–4.6 indicate that by grade O-4, inventory and authorizations are more closely tied.

Likewise, Figures 4.7 and 4.8 show relatively tumultuous patterns of inventory among O-1 and O-2 aviators. Figure 4.9 shows that it took several years for inventory to catch up with increasing authorizations (and actually decreased before they matched authorizations). Figures 4.10–4.12 indicate that authorizations and inventory are more closely matched and follow more steady patterns among the senior grades, although there have been recent slight excesses of aviator O-4s and O-5s and persistent excesses of O-6s.

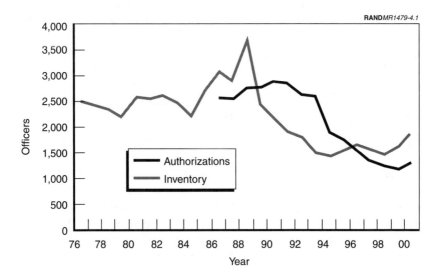

Figure 4.1—Surface Warfare Officers (O-1), Authorizations and Inventory

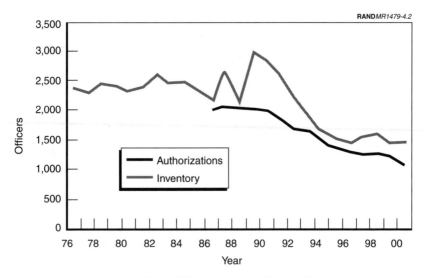

Figure 4.2—Surface Warfare Officers (O-2), Authorizations and Inventory

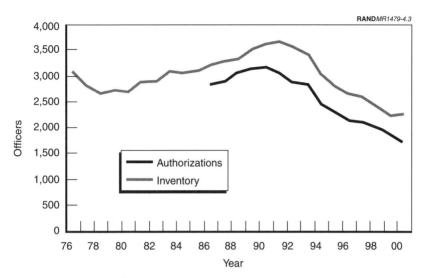

Figure 4.3—Surface Warfare Officers (O-3), Authorizations and Inventory

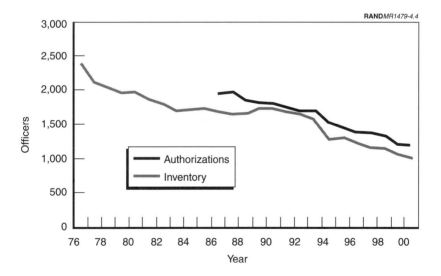

Figure 4.4—Surface Warfare Officers (O-4), Authorizations and Inventory

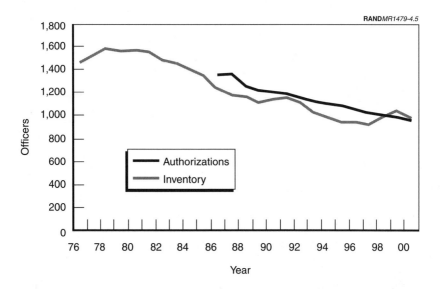

Figure 4.5—Surface Warfare Officers (O-5), Authorizations and Inventory

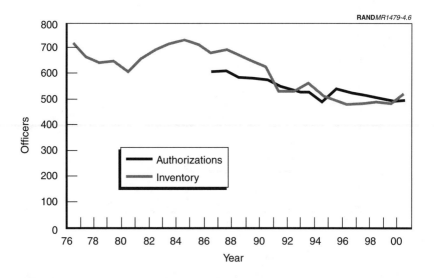

Figure 4.6—Surface Warfare Officers (O-6), Authorizations and Inventory

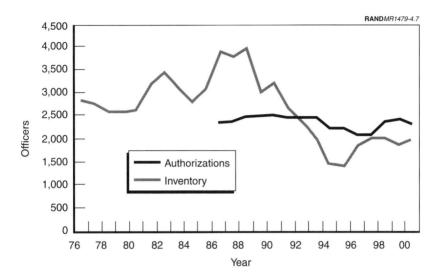

Figure 4.7—Aviation Officers (O-1), Authorizations and Inventory

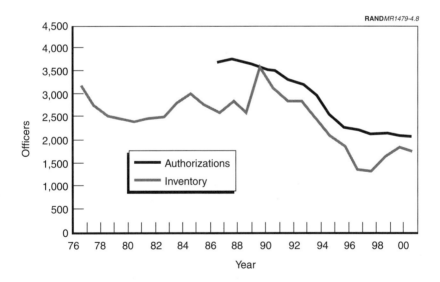

Figure 4.8—Aviation Officers (O-2), Authorizations and Inventory

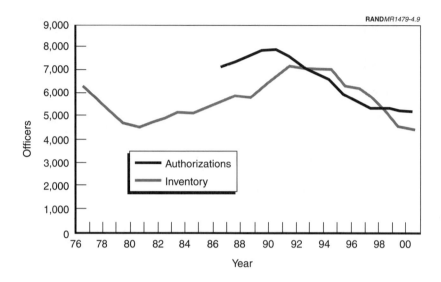

Figure 4.9—Aviation Officers (O-3), Authorizations and Inventory

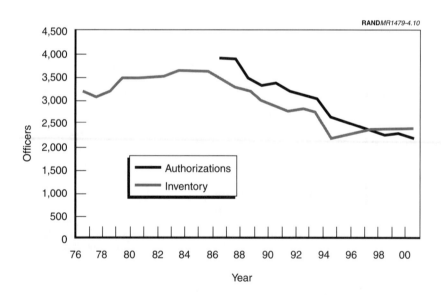

Figure 4.10—Aviation Officers (O-4), Authorizations and Inventory

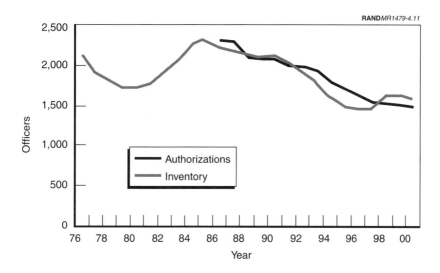

Figure 4.11—Aviation Officers (O-5), Authorizations and Inventory

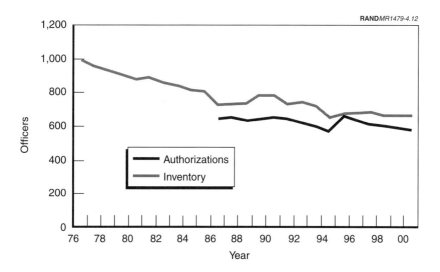

Figure 4.12—Aviation Officers (O-6), Authorizations and Inventory

Force Structure Changes Affect Gaps

Force structure changes do alter the numbers of authorizations in an effort to bring inventory in line with authorizations. While this analysis could be supported with other communities, we chose the submarine community to demonstrate this interaction between force structure, authorizations, and inventory. As discussed earlier, authorization changes can be instantaneous, while inventory change is much slower. Figures 4.13–4.18 show the authorizations and inventory of submarine officers (112x and 117x) as well as the number of submarines (both diesel- and nuclear-powered) in the fleet. The relationship between force structure changes and authorization increases and decreases is evident in these figures. Upon examination of the resulting changes to inventory, however, these data indicate the effect of a closed, cohort-based system. As these figures display, the number of junior officers can be increased relatively rapidly to respond to force structure changes and increases in authorizations, whereas increasing the numbers in more senior grades can be a more difficult and slow process. Figure 4.13 shows the steep increase of O-1s in 1984. Figure 4.14 reflects the promotion of these officers to grade O-2 in 1986. In Figure 4.15, O-3 inventory finally increases above authorizations in the latter half of the 1980s; however, the O-4 inventory indicates a perpetual shortage, and the O-5 inventory did not match authorizations until the mid-1990s, after the submarine fleet numbers had decreased for a decade. Likewise, the inventory of O-6 submarine officers did not surpass the authorizations until the late 1990s.

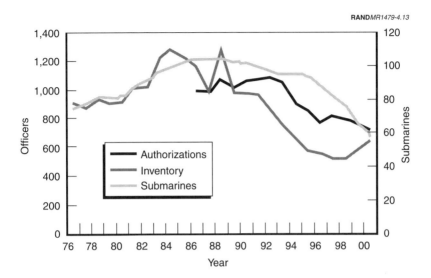

Figure 4.13—Submarine Officers (O-1), Authorizations and Inventory

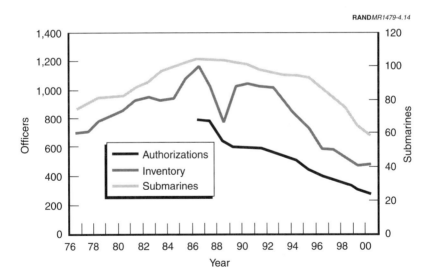

Figure 4.14—Submarine Officers (O-2), Authorizations and Inventory

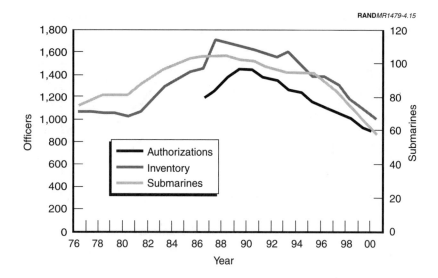

Figure 4.15—Submarine Officers (O-3), Authorizations and Inventory

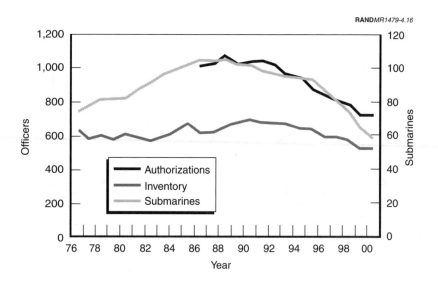

Figure 4.16—Submarine Officers (O-4), Authorizations and Inventory

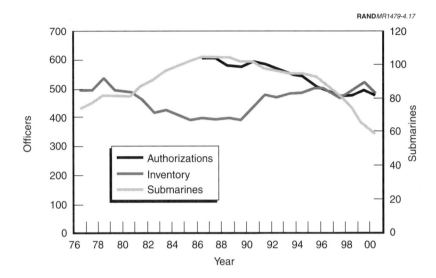

Figure 4.17—Submarine Officers (O-5), Authorizations and Inventory

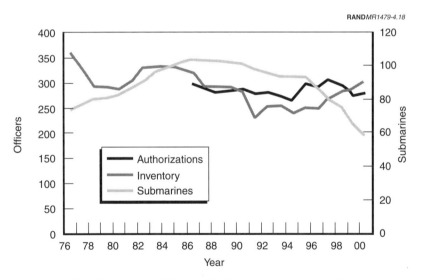

Figure 4.18—Submarine Officers (O-6), Authorizations and Inventory

External Constraints and Internal Behaviors Affect Gaps

Force structure does not explain all patterns in authorizations and inventory. In some communities, the gaps between inventory and authorizations result from competing internal demands and behaviors working contrary to pressures or controls external to the community. This is evident in the recent history of the Navy nursing community (officer designator 290x) as shown in Figures 4.19–4.24.[5]

The Nurse Corps lacks a history of senior officers. Before 1967, women were generally restricted from holding grades at or above O-5. Most nurses were women and thus were subject to these restrictions and tended to retire at or below grade O-5, or, more frequently, they left service at or before grade O-3. In the 1980s, the services revisited their requirements for nurses, and the Navy convened a medical blue-ribbon panel in 1989, which resulted in some increases in field-grade requirements for nurses.

However, the DOPMA grade-table system includes all officers (except doctors and dentists) in the same grade table and restricts the number of field-grade officers overall. Because DOPMA sets the number of field-grade officers but permits promotion timing and opportunity to float, the services are able to interpret and manage their officer communities individually. This has resulted in a zero-sum environment, in which promotions for nurses or other staff of restricted line communities are perceived to "take" promotions from the unrestricted line. In 1992, the Navy acknowledged that there were still insufficient field-grade positions for Navy nurses to prevent "promotion stagnation" even though nurses had more than their "fair share" from the DOPMA grade table. The Navy did not, at that time, intend to increase the senior grade authorizations for nurses.

In the mid-1990s, several things occurred that changed authorizations for nurses. First, the decreasing number of naval officers increased the percentage of officers they could have in senior grades. This permitted an increase in authorizations for more senior nurses without "taking" these promotions from the line. There was also a change to a different DOPMA grade table in 1997, with specific con-

---

[5]This discussion is largely excerpted from Rostker, Thie, et al. (1993), which captures this history in much greater detail (pp. 44–63).

gressional guidance that the Navy was to use the increased numbers to accommodate the Nurse Corps. These increased authorizations appear in Figures 4.23 and 4.24.

On the inventory side, the number of nurses in senior grades increased throughout this period, irrespective of the constrained authorizations. Nurses with education and experience chose to stay in the Navy and thus were eligible and appropriate for promotion to the senior ranks. This was exacerbated by the increased requirement for O-3 nurses in the early 1980s, which resulted in a cohort group movement through the field-grade ranks. These inventory develop-ments prompted the external changes to the system that resulted in the congressional guidance but that were happening irrespective of the external changes. Figure 4.22 thus shows the large cohort of nurses at grade O-4 around 1990. Figure 4.23 shows the increase in O-5 nurses as a result of promotion from the large O-4 inventory. In the case of O-6s (Figure 4.24), these authorizations still prove insuf-ficient to accommodate the large cohort moving through the system.

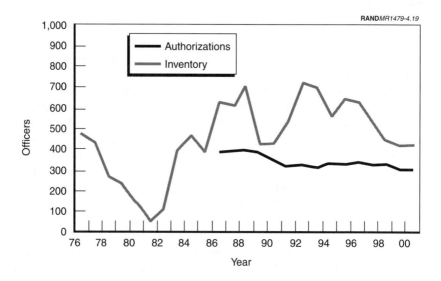

Figure 4.19—Nurses (O-1), Authorizations and Inventory

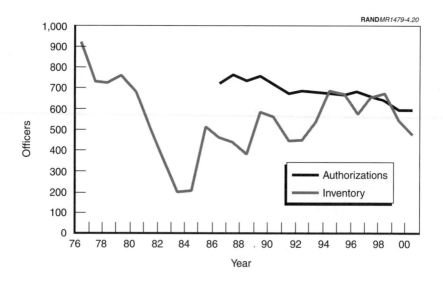

Figure 4.20—Nurses (O-2), Authorizations and Inventory

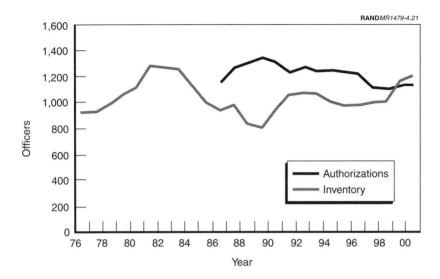

Figure 4.21—Nurses (O-3), Authorizations and Inventory

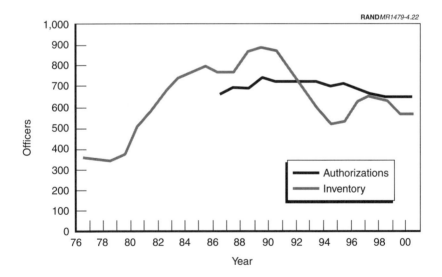

Figure 4.22—Nurses (O-4), Authorizations and Inventory

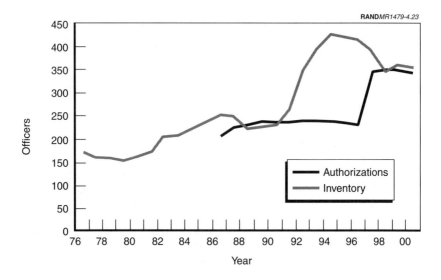

Figure 4.23—Nurses (O-5), Authorizations and Inventory

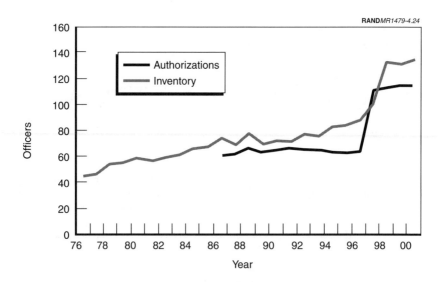

Figure 4.24—Nurses (O-6), Authorizations and Inventory

Medical Doctors Are Not Sized Against the Force Structure or Constrained by DOPMA

The medical community is not constrained by the DOPMA grade tables, and thus the behavior within the community is almost entirely cohort based. Additionally, because the Navy medical community is sized to support both the active-duty Navy personnel and their families as well as retirees, most Navy medical doctors cannot be directly associated with force structure. Thus in an environment of force structure reductions, the warfighting communities sometimes complain that the Navy medical community has not experienced greater reductions. Decreases in the medical community would likely result in greater costs through other medical coverage. While this is a possible option, decreases in the medical community beyond 5 percent require the approval of the Secretary of Defense, and reductions greater than 10 percent must be vetted through Congress.[6]

Figures 4.25–4.28 indicate the authorizations and inventory patterns for medical doctors (designators 19xx, 200x, and 210x). These data indicate that there have been reductions in medical community authorizations. In the case of doctors at grade O-5, there was excess inventory in the late 1990s. This is likely a result of the increased inventory of O-4s, which peaked in the early 1990s.

---

[6]Section 546 of the FY 1996 National Defense Authorization Act places limitations on reductions with respect to health care personnel.

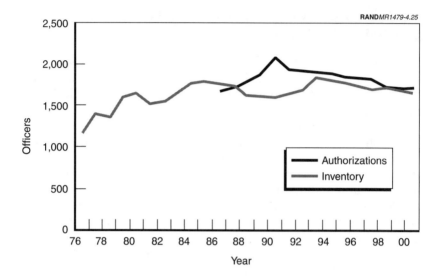

Figure 4.25—Medical Doctors (O-3), Authorizations and Inventory

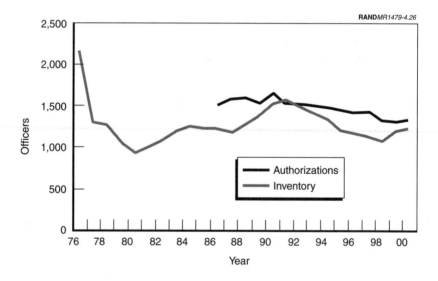

Figure 4.26—Medical Doctors (O-4), Authorizations and Inventory

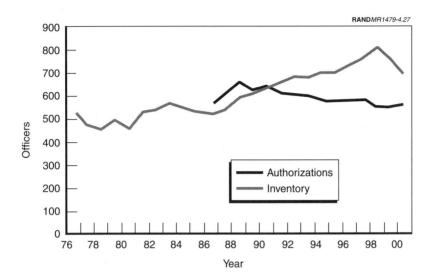

Figure 4.27—Medical Doctors (O-5), Authorizations and Inventory

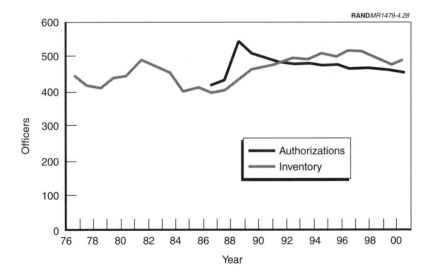

Figure 4.28—Medical Doctors (O-6), Authorizations and Inventory

Cohort Patterns Evident—but More Expensive—Among Navy Dentists

Like Navy doctors, Navy dentists are also not constrained by the DOPMA grade tables, and thus cohort-based patterns will dominate in the analysis of this community. However, unlike doctors, dentists are more closely associated with the Navy force structure, given that they serve only active-duty personnel and a small number of families (those stationed overseas). Figures 4.29–4.32 show the manpower trends for Navy dentists (220x), grades O-3 to O-6. The dentist data show the results of downsizing authorizations while larger cohorts are still moving through the system. Figure 4.29 indicates a decreasing inventory of junior dentists, consistent with decreasing authorizations. However, the relative peak of dentists occurs when those who were O-3s in 1986–1988 were promoted to O-4 in the early 1990s (Figure 4.30), despite the decreasing authorizations at that grade. This also explains the peak in O-5s at the end of the 1990s (Figure 4.31) and likely explains the upward trend of O-6s (Figure 4.32). These patterns mimic those seen in the surface warfare and submarine communities. However, those unrestricted line communities enter officers at grade O-1 and suffer wide cohort swings at the junior grades but generally reduce the gaps in the more senior grades. Because dentists enter at grade O-3, the cohort swings occur at the more expensive paygrades in this community.

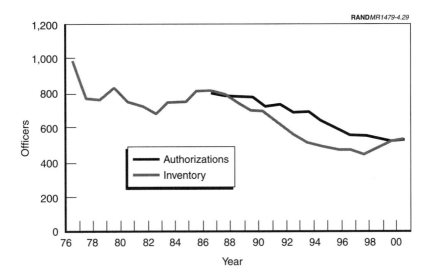

Figure 4.29—Dentists (O-3), Authorizations and Inventory

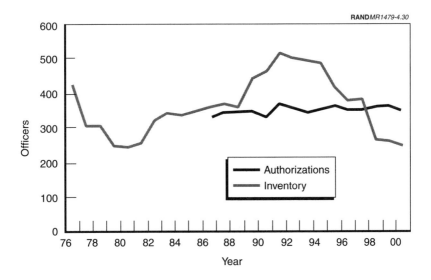

Figure 4.30—Dentists (O-4), Authorizations and Inventory

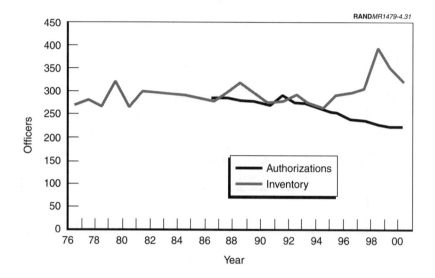

Figure 4.31—Dentists (O-5), Authorizations and Inventory

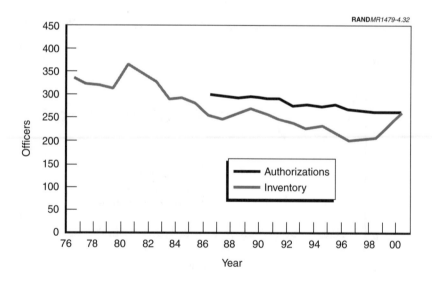

Figure 4.32—Dentists (O-6), Authorizations and Inventory

The Grade Structure of a Community Affects Gaps

Figures 4.33–4.38 indicate the historical authorization and inventory levels of supply officers (designator 31xx). Despite shortages until recently in grade O-1 and perpetual overages in grade O-2, the inventory of this community has tracked closely with its authorizations. Part of the explanation for why some communities, such as this one, minimize gaps while others have perpetual manning overages or shortages rests in the grade structure of the community.

Figure 4.39 shows the grade structures for selected communities. This graph indicates the percentage of BA for that community at each grade, as of 2000. The supply community grade structure differs notably from the other communities. Despite the consistent decreases in O-1 authorizations (as per Figure 4.33), O-1s still have a relatively large share of BA compared with O-2s. While the O-1 authorizations for the unrestricted line communities also exceed O-2 authorizations, those communities tend to experience greater numbers of transfers to other communities and thus need a relatively larger O-1 inventory. Therefore, the relative proportion of supply O-1 and O-2 authorizations likely explains the history of O-1 shortages and O-2 overages among supply officers. Of greater note for the supply community, however, is the lack of gaps in grades O-3 to O-6. The spike to O-3 authorizations is attainable for most communities because officers remain in grade at O-3 considerably longer than at O-1 or O-2. However, many officers leave the Navy as O-3s. The relative drop between O-3 and O-4 authorizations is key to the supply community being able to manage its manning. In contrast, the submarine, surface warfare, and intelligence communities have force structures that are very difficult to satisfy, absent dramatic increases in O-3 retention, or much longer service at grade O-4 (which would disrupt the ability to meet O-5 authorizations). The supply community also has a relatively high promotion opportunity to O-5, which likely motivates retention without resulting in overages at the senior grades. The relative proportion of O-4 to O-5 within the supply community contrasts with the pattern of those grades among doctors. Given the shape of the doctor structure, it is not surprising that Figures 4.27 and 4.28 showed inventory overages for senior doctors; the grade structure is not manageable in the current system that emphasizes maintaining reasonable promotion opportunity for all officers.

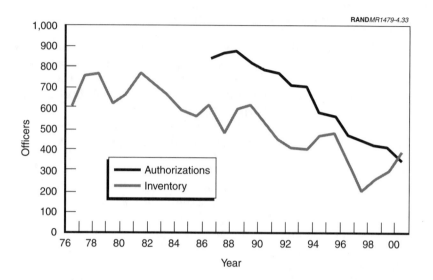

Figure 4.33—Supply Officers (O-1), Authorizations and Inventory

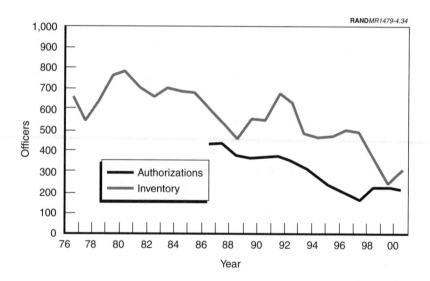

Figure 4.34—Supply Officers (O-2), Authorizations and Inventory

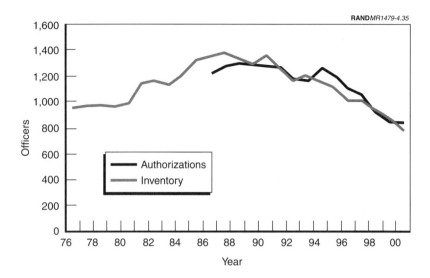

Figure 4.35—Supply Officers (O-3), Authorizations and Inventory

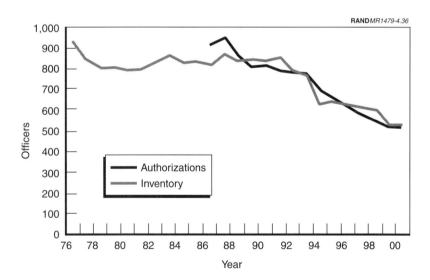

Figure 4.36—Supply Officers (O-4), Authorizations and Inventory

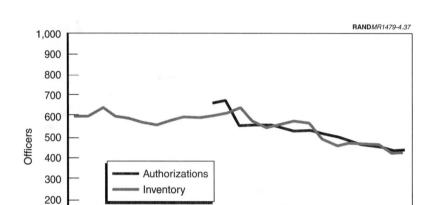

Figure 4.37—Supply Officers (O-5), Authorizations and Inventory

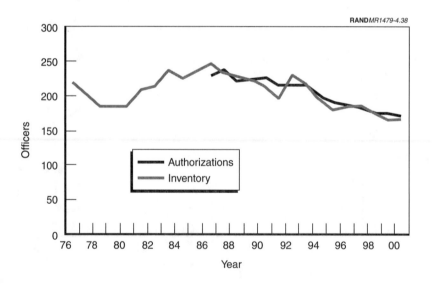

Figure 4.38—Supply Officers (O-6), Authorizations and Inventory

The intelligence community also has a unique but problematic grade structure, evident in Figure 4.39, which results in management struggles and the gaps displayed in Figures 4.40–4.45. The relative proportion of O-3 to O-4 authorizations would present a difficult challenge in meeting O-4 in any community. However, the perpetual O-3 shortages in this community (Figure 4.42) make it even more difficult to close the gap at O-4. Inventory shortages are also evident at the more senior grades and are generally exacerbated by a grade structure in which the proportion of O-6 billets is close to that of O-1 billets.

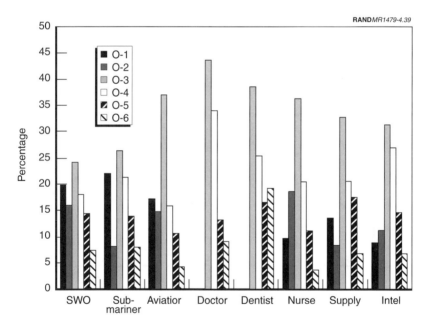

**Figure 4.39—Proportionate Grade Structure of
Selected Communities, 2000**

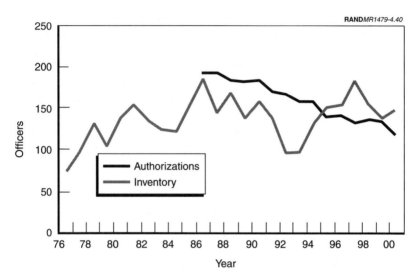

Figure 4.40—Intelligence Officers (O-1), Authorizations and Inventory

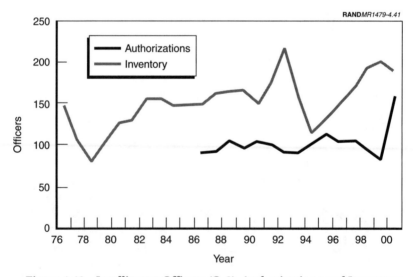

Figure 4.41—Intelligence Officers (O-2), Authorizations and Inventory

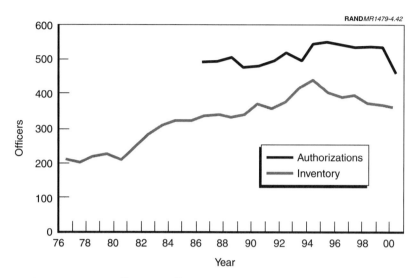

Figure 4.42—Intelligence Officers (O-3), Authorizations and Inventory

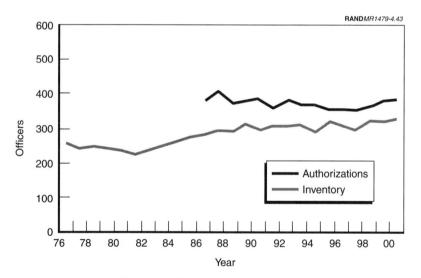

Figure 4.43—Intelligence Officers (O-4), Authorizations and Inventory

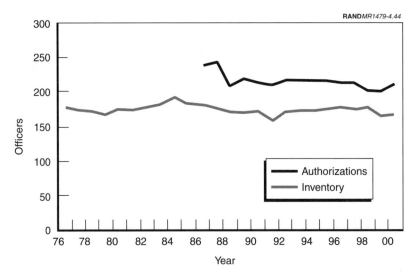

Figure 4.44—Intelligence Officers (O-5), Authorizations and Inventory

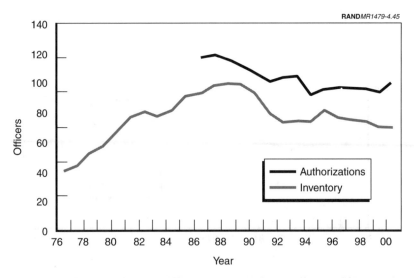

Figure 4.45—Intelligence Officers (O-6), Authorizations and Inventory

FACTORS THAT CONTRIBUTE TO MANPOWER GAPS

In sum, any gap analysis of military manpower needs to examine each community individually because there are multiple reasons for communities to experience manning shortages or excesses at various grades. The system can react most quickly to large-scale changes at the junior grades. Thus, these grades are likely to show the greatest fluctuation in inventory. However, large fluctuations result in varying sizes of cohort groups moving through the system. While external constraints or controls can affect the level of authorizations within communities, these cohorts will present management hurdles. Finally, the grade structures of some communities are inherently easier to manage. Some grade structures suggest perpetual overages, such as with senior doctors; other communities, such as the submarine community, are locked into almost unattainable grade structures. The latter suggests the need for a reevaluation of the proportionate grade structure for such communities.

Chapter Five

GAP ANALYSIS COSTING

Both hard costs and soft costs are associated with manning overages and shortages. *Hard costs* are more easily identified and include dollar costs or savings associated with compensation—and accession and training costs. *Soft costs* are more difficult to identify and quantify. Examples of soft costs include lower performance due to training, motivation, or other deficiencies; readiness problems due to uncompleted work or low retention; and low workforce task cohesion due to instability among a crew. In the short term, these soft costs are measured by elements other than dollars, if measured at all.

As Figure 5.1 indicates, the hard costs of gaps can increase or decrease, based on the size and nature of the difference between inventory and authorizations. For example, if a force is overmanned (having more inventory than authorizations), the hard costs are higher because unneeded personnel are brought in, trained, and compensated. If a force is undermanned (having less inventory than authorizations), there is likely to be a savings in hard costs because there are fewer people than planned. However, this simple calculation ignores the costs of lost production because needed work is forgone. This cost is not as easily measured and is often ameliorated by the workforce laboring longer hours than planned to accomplish the tasks. Also, depending on the nature of the undermanning, average cost efficiency may be lowered if higher-ranking or more-highly trained individuals are being paid to perform tasks that are normally the responsibility of lower-ranking or less-highly trained individuals.

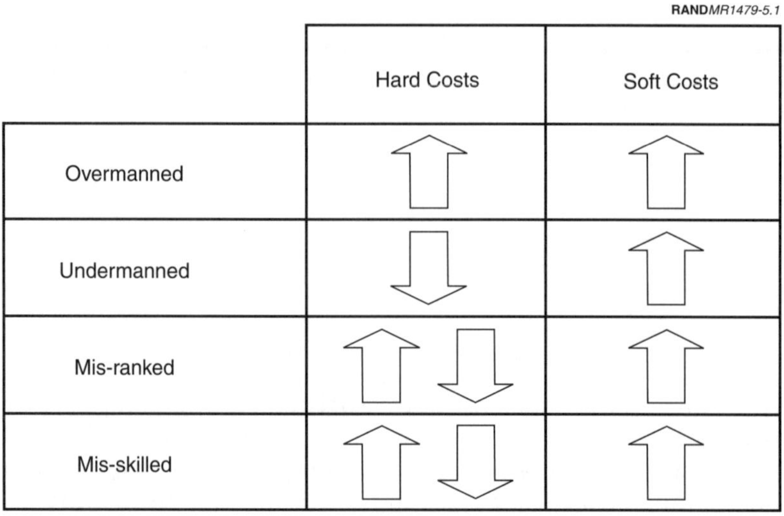

RAND*MR1479-5.1*

	Hard Costs	Soft Costs
Overmanned	⬆	⬆
Undermanned	⬇	⬆
Mis-ranked	⬆ ⬇	⬆
Mis-skilled	⬆ ⬇	⬆

Figure 5.1—Relationship Between Hard Costs/Soft Costs and Manpower Discrepancies

If a force is *mis-ranked*—the correct number of officers but not the correct distribution of grades—then the hard costs will vary depending on the characteristics of the grade differences. If given a constant number of individuals—an excess of junior personnel and a shortage of senior personnel—the overall dollar cost of the system will decrease, and the average cost per person will also decrease. This is a savings from what was planned. However, soft costs also exist but are not as easily measured. For example, the ability of the less experienced personnel to perform the duties required is not assured, and morale will likely suffer because of leadership shortages and a resulting inability of leadership to devote time to guidance, training, and mentoring. Additionally, junior personnel will likely be expected to perform the duties and responsibilities of more senior officers. Making such demands of junior officers for more than a short period, without providing additional compensation and rewards, is likely to have a negative effect on morale, performance, and retention.

Should the system have an excess of senior officers and a shortage of junior officers, the hard costs will reverse to a system more expensive overall and more expensive per individual than what had been planned. However, such a system would be more productive and more effective per individual.[1] However, to the extent that the requirements of the system truly indicate a need for junior officers and that the duties and responsibilities of the billets are those associated with junior officers, then there will also likely be morale problems resulting from senior officers who feel their expertise and experience are underused. Morale problems are especially likely to occur to the extent that some of the duties normally performed by junior officers, such as standing watch, are less appealing to senior officers.

If a system is *mis-skilled*—the correct number of officers but not distributed in the correct occupations—then the resulting cost overall and on average will vary depending on whether there is a disproportionate excess or shortage of highly trained technical personnel. An excess would increase hard costs, and a shortage would lead to savings. However, a mis-skilled force is likely to suffer considerable soft costs. In some instances, individuals may be compelled to perform outside their area of training or to work extra duty within their areas to compensate for a shortage of personnel with their training. Additionally, if a skill area is overmanned, then individuals with that skill may not have the opportunity to develop their skills and perform as they would expect. Any such skill mismatches are likely to have negative morale and readiness effects, which are difficult to quantify, but which we recognize here as soft costs.

In sum, the nature of the manning difference, whether the force is over- or undermanned, mis-ranked, or mis-skilled, may have cost or savings implications in hard dollars. In contrast, the soft costs, which are more difficult to quantify, are likely to increase in any circumstance of manning difference. While undermanning in particular will generally produce short-term budget savings, the long-term cost consequences of persistent undermanning, mis-ranking, and mis-skilling will eventually appear.

---

[1]See, for example, Gary R. Nelson, Robert M. Gay, and Charles Robert Roll, Jr., *Manpower Cost Reduction in Electronics Maintenance: Framework and Recommendations,* Santa Monica, Calif.: RAND, R-1483-ARPA, July 1974.

DOLLAR COSTS OF MANPOWER GAPS

This section provides the dollar costs for the manpower differences evident in the earlier figures of Chapter Four. These figures convey a somewhat different perspective than one gained by just netting manpower numbers as if all grades and occupations were equal. The net overages and shortages are weighted by the different costs of an officer to produce a grade or an occupation cost and give a more accurate picture of what it means to have a particular shortage or overage. In essence, a high-cost grade or occupation magnifies the costs and savings to the Navy.

There are several sources of Navy manpower costs, each of which meets specific users' needs. Navy personnel who manage officer communities generally use standard programming rates that give a single dollar figure (typically the average Military Personnel, Navy [MPN] for all Navy officers) for an officer regardless of grade or skill. This figure is used in the programming process where manpower is typically programmed in units of end strength. Composite Standard Military Rates provide officer costs (average MPN costs) differentiated by grade and are typically used for estimating reimbursable costs. VAMOSC (Visibility and Management of Operating and Support Costs) provides historical personnel (MPN) costs by units (ships, squadrons, etc.). For our analysis, we use costs determined by the Naval Center for Cost Analysis' COMET[2] (Cost of Manpower Estimating Tool) model that develops costs by officer grade and skill. COMET provides both direct[3] and indirect[4] manning costs. These numbers are shown in Table 5.1. As evident in the table data, these communities could be arranged into three cost groups—low, medium, and high. In the low-cost group, we include fleet support, Medical Service Corps, intelligence, cryptology, civil engineer, and Nurse Corps; LDO, SWO, and supply reside in the medium-cost

---

[2]The COMET model, along with extensive documentation and data files, is available at www.ncca.navy.mil/comet.

[3]Direct costs include military compensation, housing and subsistence allowances, moving costs, retired pay accrual, special and incentive pays, and other benefits paid to the officer.

[4]Indirect (MPN) costs include (the average per-officer costs) for recruiting, initial training, locating (individuals), medical/dental, base support, and administration.

Table 5.1

Manpower Costs by Grade, Selected Communities (FY01$)

Designator	Community	Paygrade						
		O-1	O-2	O-3	O-4	O-5	O-6	
1110	Surface Warfare Officer	88,122	104,405	122,334	138,953	158,210	184,192	
1120	Submariner	129,301	147,247	168,722	184,027	202,756	227,442	
1310	Pilot	130,095	145,382	164,511	180,229	202,538	228,659	
1320	Naval Flight Officer	131,048	146,484	165,606	181,989	203,876	228,430	
1610	Cryptologic	74,092	87,509	105,008	121,039	140,723	161,874	
1630	Intelligence	72,273	87,908	103,420	117,932	140,071	165,413	
1700	Fleet Support	68,944	86,700	102,715	117,699	136,165	160,349	
2100	Doctor	105,454	N/A	166,386	183,944	201,074	224,032	
2200	Dentist	110,556	N/A	127,818	155,129	175,407	202,603	
2300	Medical Service Corps	74,270	86,820	102,614	117,575	136,888	162,664	
2900	Nurse Corps	72,810	86,595	103,460	115,187	137,884	167,114	
3100	Supply Corps	90,409	106,081	122,678	136,777	156,456	179,149	
5100	Civil Engineer Corps	71,851	86,985	103,018	118,151	138,946	168,722	
6000	Limited Duty Officer	82,445	95,203	115,099	129,931	149,655	185,991	

group; and the high-cost group includes submariners, pilots, naval flight officers, and doctors. Dentists straddle the medium- and high-cost groups.

Figure 5.2 provides the cost of the manpower gaps for selected communities over time, based on the costs shown in Table 5.1. For this chart and subsequent ones like it, we have subtracted authorizations from inventory and then calculated the cost of the difference. A positive number means a dollar cost as described above and a negative number means a dollar savings as described above. (We are ignoring what we have previously defined as soft costs.) In this figure, the surface warfare community (in the aggregate) has cost more than planned because of its overmanning for most of the time period. Re-examining the earlier gap figures for the surface warfare community reveals that in 2000 all grades except O-4 had more officers than authorized. (The current personnel management system may be the root cause of such patterns. Frequently, because of long-standing shortages at grade O-4, the system compensates by accessing more officers than otherwise needed in the hope that, 10 years later, the O-1 will become an O-4. Given the manning needs on ships, however, it may not be feasible to provide all the officers satisfactory experience.)

At the other extreme, the aviation community has (in the aggregate) cost less than planned (saved dollars) because of its undermanning for most of the time period. (Again, we are ignoring the costs of forgone work and training.) There are fewer officers than authorized. The shortages tend to be consistently at grades O-1 and O-2 (and more recently at grade O-3), while the overages consistently are at the high-cost grade O-6 and recently at grades O-4 and O-5 as well. Currently, personnel rules that promote officers to higher grades at certain points in time are irrespective of whether more officers in those grades may be needed. The Navy appears to be using more senior officers either to fly planes in lieu of more junior officers or to be using these senior officers as excess staff or to staff disproportionately 1000/1050 billets. Either way, the savings from not having junior officers are reduced by having too many senior officers. Moreover, such long-standing "savings" should prompt the question whether these missing officers are needed at all, or if they existed,

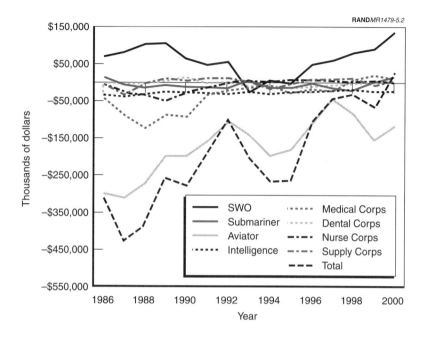

Figure 5.2—Dollar Costs (+) or Savings (–) Resulting from Manpower Gaps (inventory minus authorizations) in Selected Communities (constant FY01$)

whether they would be affordable. Also, the entire system, year by year, nets its costs and savings to an overall savings, which indicates that having fewer pilots than planned each year helps to fund the inefficiencies elsewhere in the system, particularly for SWOs.

Because the range of costs/savings are bounded on the upper side by the surface warfare community and on the lower side by the aviation community, Figure 5.3 once again shows these cost/savings trends, omitting aviation and surface warfare (and also omitting them from the total), to provide greater detail. With the exception of the intelligence community and Medical Corps, most communities cycle in a narrow band around the $0 gridline. Sometimes they cost and sometimes they save, but in general they are within a likely management tolerance, which is not inconsistent with the friction of managing inventory in a closed system, discussed earlier. The intelligence community, which has seen relatively little change in its chronic undermanning, consistently has "savings"—fewer dollar costs than planned. However, the Medical Corps has decreased its long-standing undermanning and currently costs slightly more than planned. Averaged together, the six communities shown in Figure 5.3 have become more costly to the Navy each year since 1988 (in essence, the savings disappear over time) as undermanning, especially in the highest-cost medical community, has been reduced.

Figures 5.4–5.11 provide a more detailed presentation of each selected community and indicate costs/savings by differences at each grade in the community as well as the total associated with differences in that community.

Figure 5.4 indicates the dramatic upward trend of costs—since 1993 in the surface warfare community—associated with manning

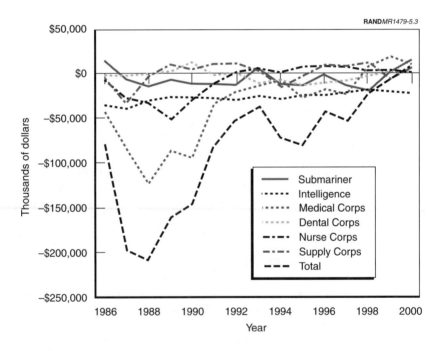

Figure 5.3—Dollar Costs or Savings Resulting from Manpower Gap in Selected Communities, Excluding Surface Warfare and Aviation (constant FY01$)

overages in that community, especially at the junior grades. While the junior grades cost less, the large numbers in excess of need make high accessions a costly practice. Moreover, grade O-3 is consistently overmanned, while grade O-4 is consistently undermanned. The need in this community to bring dollar costs into balance appears to be for fewer officers overall but more at grade O-4. There are perverse solutions as well: Increasing O-5 and O-6 while reducing O-1 to O-3 would bring the system into cost balance but would exacerbate the soft costs discussed earlier; simply decreasing O-5 and O-6 would offset the cost of the higher number of O-1 and O-2 but would also exacerbate soft costs if the higher-graded officers were truly needed. A useful solution is to find ways to provide officers experience more quickly, in which case O-3s might have sufficient experience to fill some of what are now O-4 billets, and thus O-4 authorizations could decrease.

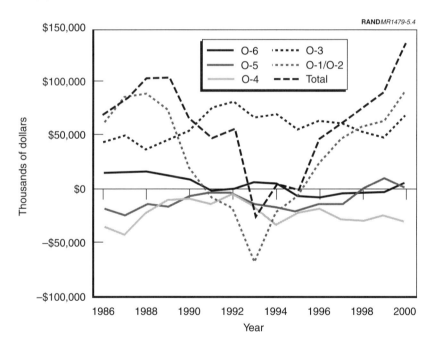

Figure 5.4—Dollar Costs or Savings Resulting from Surface Warfare
Community Manpower Gap, by Grade (constant FY01$)

As a whole, as shown in Figure 5.5, the submarine community appears to keep costs/savings within a reasonable band. The higher costs associated with overmanning O-1 to O-3 are offset by the savings associated with the chronic undermanning at O-4. It is unclear, however, whether there are abnormal soft costs from junior officers doing the work of more senior officers. Grade O-5 has moved toward balance, and grade O-6 has been generally balanced over time. The recent spike in costs is tied to increases in all grades except O-3.

This community (as well as aviation to be discussed) should probably have its grade structure examined. Because of the initial training costs, junior officers are very costly, and the cost of senior officers rises less than the cost of senior officers in many other communities. Put another way, it may make sense to seek greater service from trained junior officers by shifting the grade authorizations up to give earlier promotion and thus more compensation sooner. Training

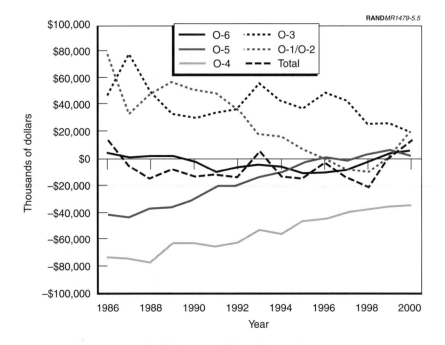

Figure 5.5—Dollar Costs or Savings Resulting from Submarine Community Manpower Gap, by Grade (constant FY01$)

fewer officers initially but keeping more of those trained through incentives may be desirable. In essence, the cost of a higher-graded authorization offsets the cost of training a new O-1. Suggestions like this type should be evaluated in more detail.

As discussed earlier, shortages in junior (O-1 and O-2) aviation officers have consistently resulted in lower-than-planned manning costs for the aviation community (Figure 5.6). Since 1994, the savings associated with paygrades O-1 to O-2 have decreased while O-3 savings have increased. This high-cost community has also experienced an overall upward cost trend since 1987, also driven by increases in O-4 and O-5 and offset by the savings at grade O-3. As shown in Table 5.1, the cost of producing an O-1 and O-2 is high, so "savings" dissipate quickly as O-1 and O-2 undermanning decreases. Moving toward meeting authorizations becomes costly. The aviation

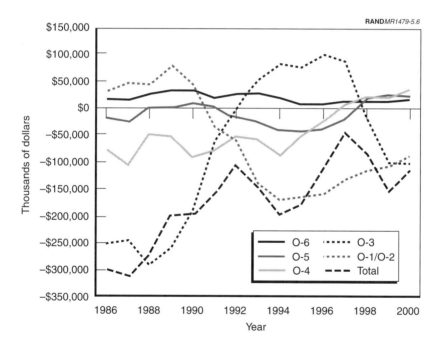

Figure 5.6—Dollar Costs or Savings Resulting from Aviation Community
Manpower Gap, by Grade (constant FY01$)

community appears to be one whose grade structure and experience patterns also should be rethought. Finding a way to keep more expensively trained officers longer (pilots currently have a more lengthy service commitment than other officers after qualification as a pilot) can be useful if it means avoiding training costs. The marginal grade-to-grade costs are small compared with the initial cost of training an officer.

So far, we have discussed costs as though they were static. In reality, the cost structure changes dynamically with other personnel management changes because of the need to increase or decrease the number of certain types of officer. Such costing is beyond the scope of this report.

Although, as shown in Figure 5.7, the annual dollar savings or costs associated with differences in the supply community have fluctuated

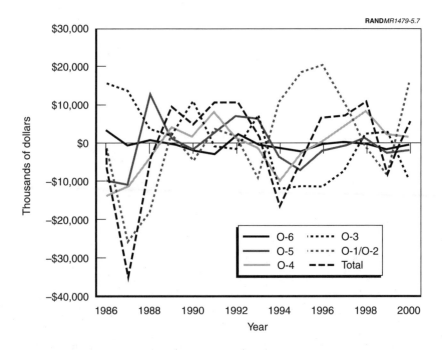

Figure 5.7—Dollar Costs or Savings Resulting from Supply Community
Manpower Gap, by Grade (constant FY01$)

from positive to negative, there is relatively little cost variation in this community compared with the others examined. Most grades, and the community overall, cycle within a reasonable tolerance.

The pattern by grade in the intelligence community is relatively consistent over time, resulting in consistent dollar savings (Figure 5.8). Are all the authorizations truly needed if they are so consistently undermanned? Perversely, removing such authorizations would increase dollar costs in the short term but would ameliorate the softer costs in the long term.

Figure 5.9 shows the costing results for doctors. As discussed previously, the community has come into balance recently, although it has represented increased dollar costs to the Navy in doing so. Other reports suggest that these costs may have been offset in other por-

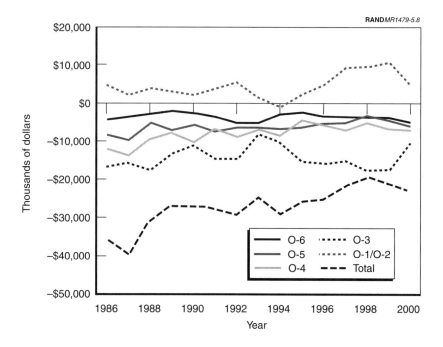

Figure 5.8—Dollar Costs or Savings Resulting from Intelligence
Community Manpower Gap, by Grade (constant FY01$)

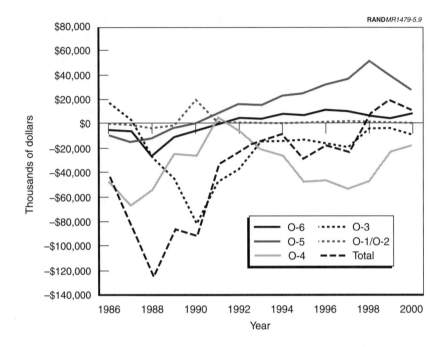

**Figure 5.9—Dollar Costs or Savings Resulting from Doctor Community
Manpower Gap, by Grade (constant FY01$)**

tions of the defense health program. The dentist community (Figure 5.10) has also recently come into cost balance. The nursing community has incurred some costs during the 1990s but more recently has shown a relatively stable pattern (Figure 5.11).

Last, we present two views for the year 2000 that summarize the previous figures and discussion. We recognize that time trends are at work, but we use this year to highlight the concepts. Figure 5.12 shows the average cost of one officer for each community as planned and as actually executed. This cost is derived by weighting the number of graded authorizations and inventory by the grade cost from

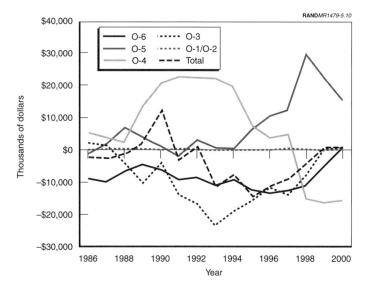

Figure 5.10—Dollar Costs or Savings Resulting from Dentist Community Manpower Gap, by Grade (constant FY01$)

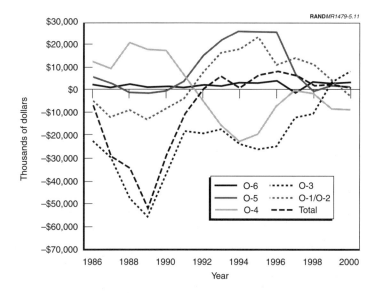

Figure 5.11—Dollar Costs or Savings Resulting from Nurse Community Manpower Gap, by Grade (constant FY01$)

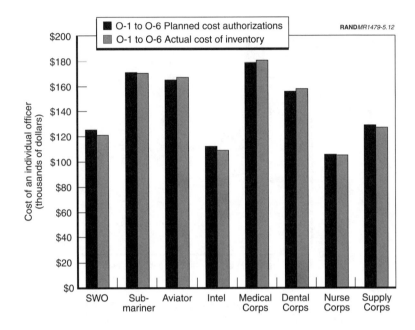

Figure 5.12—Average Cost of an Individual Officer, FY 2000

COMET (Table 5.1).[5] Differences among communities are the result of cost differences as well as grade structure differences. Differences between the two bars in Figure 5.12 represent differences between the planned cost (what the authorizations would cost) and actual inventory costs. If, as in the case of the surface warfare community, the excess inventory is equal to that of junior officers, then this excess will draw the average cost downward.

In terms of cost, not all officers are equal. On average, Medical Corps officers are the most costly officers, and nurses are the least costly. Submariners and aviators are about 35 percent more costly to enter and develop than SWOs. One difference between the communities is the source of the cost difference. For example, aviators and

_____

[5]In other words, if there are 10 officers for each grade of O-1 through O-6 in a community, then the numerator of the calculation would be 10×the cost of an O-1, 10×the cost of an O-2, etc. The denominator would be the total number of officers—60 in this case.

submariners are more expensive than SWOs because of the training costs and compensation differences at each grade. However, one of the main reasons the medical community is expensive is because doctors are primarily at higher grades. In other words, doctors are expensive because they are more highly graded; submariners and aviators are expensive because they cost more, even at junior grades, than some officers in other communities.

Given the differences, the Navy should always be looking to substitute lower-cost personnel for higher-cost personnel. In particular, unless there are valid needs, requirements for aviators and submariners, apart from ship and aviation manning documents, should be minimized. Also, assigning aviators and submariners to 1000/1050 billets should be a last choice. The availability of such officers to staff these billets indicates an oversupply of this high-priced resource.

Figure 5.13 presents the data aggregated by community. Compared with Figure 5.12, the effect of the numbers of officers in each community weights the costs to present a slightly different picture.

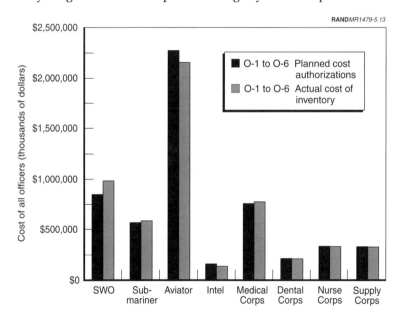

Figure 5.13—Cost of Officers by Community, FY 2000

By far the most costly community is aviation. If one wanted to expend effort on making requirements and authorizations more accurate, this is where he or she would start following the "Willie Sutton principle."[6] Moreover, it is clear that, at least in FY 2000, SWOs were costing more than authorized (through overages and mis-ranking) and aviators were costing less. Why? It may be that the entry costs of other communities were being paid by SWOs who will eventually migrate to other communities. It may be that there are too many accessions within an infeasible experiencing structure of ship billets, and new ways might be needed to train, experience, and acculturate junior officers. If the excess O-1 to O-3 officers are actually filling O-4 billets or "double filling" O-1 to O-3 billets, then there are undoubtedly high soft costs being paid as well that will affect future behaviors of individual officers. Even using rudimentary economic costs by grade and occupation, as found in COMET, allows interesting questions to be asked.

SUMMARY

In sum, manpower gaps, including deltas, differences, and mismatches, occur throughout the Navy in various patterns across different communities and in different grades. Some explanations emerge when the communities are considered individually. First, broad fluctuations are not uncommon at the junior grades, as the communities can adjust inventory more quickly at junior grades to respond to need. However, these fluctuations at junior grades create cohorts of differing sizes that move through the system and may not be in concert with the needs of the community, such as changes in requirements based on force structure. Some communities, such as the doctor community, are not tied directly to force structure, and thus their community patterns may differ even from dentists, who are tied more closely to the size of the Navy. External constraints may also affect authorizations or requirements and cause BA to be inconsistent with the inventory, as they are in the nurse community. The grade structure of the communities also plays an important role; some communities are shaped such that gaps are inevitable. In

---

[6]When asked why he robbed banks, Sutton replied simply, "That's where the money is."

short, each community must be understood separately to analyze the reasons for its manpower "gaps."

Given the existence of such gaps, it is possible to quantify dollar costs and acknowledge the probable existence of softer costs. Soft costs result from behavioral response to gaps and may lead to problems of performance, capability, readiness, and ultimately other dollar costs, such as those related to additional accession and training. The dollar costs that are more easily calculated result from the differences themselves. Like the explanation of community gaps, the costs and savings must also be considered by community and grade. Overall, however, the Navy has experienced past dollar savings as a result of manning shortfalls. But that has reversed, and the Navy is now encountering higher dollar costs as manning moves toward authorizations. However, the real unknown is whether bearing the short-term dollar costs of minimizing gaps will bear long-term fruit in the form of much reduced soft costs that could lead to future dollar savings.

Chapter Six

FUTURE REQUIREMENTS AND INVENTORY

Changes in the size and composition of the Navy's future officer force are anticipated. Dynamic factors leading to these changes include changes in the number of ships, aircraft, and submarines; technology improvements; organizational realignment; and emerging threats and changes in missions/tasks/functions. Force structure changes occur as ships, aircraft, and submarines enter and leave service. Also, as new hardware and equipment come on line, there is pressure to operate new platforms with reduced manning, and therefore reduce the overall life-cycle costs of these platforms.

This chapter examines, briefly and retrospectively, the Navy's past accuracy in predicting changes to the officer manpower system. Recognizing the inherent weaknesses in forecasting such manpower changes, we nonetheless discuss potential reasons the Navy manpower requirements might change in size or in composition (grade and designator); we then posit possible future manpower requirements for 2010 and 2017. The years were chosen by the research sponsor, and the manpower scenarios for each are intended as an analytical underpinning to examine the Navy's ability to respond with manning changes to meet changing requirements. Our estimates are not intended to serve as the basis for further planning beyond 2017. Given these officer manpower scenarios, this chapter discusses what such an officer manpower structure would look like, by grade and designator. The next chapter will discuss steady-state and transitional issues in managing officers to meet such a set of authorizations.

THE WEAKNESS OF FORECASTING EFFORTS

Inherent difficulties plague any effort to forecast manpower. The Navy manpower system revisits its five-year forecasts by revising OPAs three times a year. N-12 conducts these revisions by extending the current manpower numbers into the future to reflect the Navy program, which has a special emphasis on force structure. A comparison of the actual authorizations during the forecast periods with the forecasted numbers indicates that forecasts tend to reflect current trends; however, they cannot accurately predict the future manpower requirements. Figure 6.1, which shows the error rate (mean absolute deviation) of the OPA forecasts examined in this work, demonstrates that manpower projections become especially difficult in the third to fifth year of projection and that this pattern is consistent across communities. We include OPA predictions and actual authorizations for selected Navy communities in Appendix A.

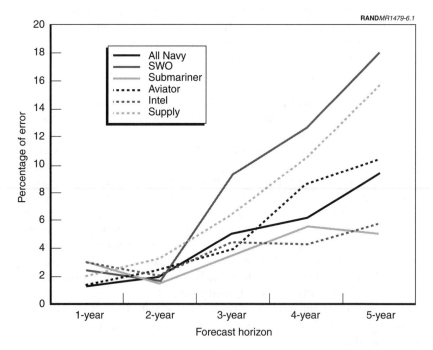

Figure 6.1—Average Forecasting Errors: OPA Predictions by Community

FUTURE REQUIREMENTS SCENARIOS: AN ANALYTICAL EXERCISE

This analysis identifies and posits the effect of dynamic changes to the naval officer community for years 2010 and 2017. We developed these scenarios as analytical exercises to explore the ability of the officer force to adapt to such changes.

To develop the future naval officer force for years 2010 and 2017, we used Navy planning documents to evaluate recent trends in the officer structure and also used the project team's best judgment on the effect of dynamic factors on officer manpower. Navy planning documents provided historical and future officer manpower projection—that is, billets the Navy bought and future trends in the officer structure that the Navy intends to fund. A DMDC database provided historical OPA—that is, billets that the Navy funded and programmed authorizations through FY 2005. In addition to these trends, we estimated the effects of several dynamic factors that are expected to cause changes to the officer structure. These factors include force structure changes, emerging technology, and manpower changes to joint activities, which are discussed in detail below.

We sorted the DMDC database into two major categories, operational forces and support forces.[1] Dividing by this method allowed for an evaluation of trends, primarily between forces assigned at sea and those who directly support them (operational forces), and all others (support forces). This methodology was useful in that it allowed the research team to apply its best judgment to posit the impact of future changes to operational forces (changes in numbers of

---

[1]The elements of the database included billets authorized by FYDP major program codes, which were comprised of 11 major programs. Major program codes are outlined in DoD 7045.7-H, November 2000. The 11 codes are, in order, Strategic Forces; General Purpose Forces; Command, Control, Communications, Intelligence and Space; Mobility Forces; Guard and Reserve Forces; Research and Development; Central Supply and Maintenance; Training, Medical, and Other General Personnel Activities; Administration and Associated Activities; Support of Other Nations; and Special Operations Forces. For the purposes of our analysis, the FYDP major programs that comprised operational forces were Strategic Forces, General Purpose Forces, and Special Operations Forces. This is consistent with the tooth-to-tail data we discussed earlier (Figure 3.27) and with the Navy's designation of combat and support forces (*Total Force Manpower Management System (TFMMS) Coding Directory*, NAVPERS 16000A, January 2001).

units and ships) and support force (changes as a result of Base Realignment and Closure [BRAC], outsourcing, and privatization)
structure on officer manpower.

The future officer profile from 2010 to 2017 was developed by con-
sidering the extent of transformation the Navy could perform by
replacement of its legacy ships, submarines, aircraft, weapons, and
systems. The Navy in 2017 will still consist of a significant number of
ships, submarines, and aircraft that are currently under construction
or in the fleet today. However, future systems manpower will reflect
the incremental effects of long-term manpower reduction trends.
The research team assessed that several dynamic factors would affect
naval officer manpower for 2017 and include changes to force structure, organizational structure, functional requirements, and the use
of emerging technologies. These factors are inextricably linked, and
the dynamic and combined effects were posited to change future
officer requirements, with their effects varying by community. In
addition, rapid increases in technology and the need for greater integration will shift the emphasis of the unrestricted line from operating
platforms to integrating them and will support the creation for the
new naval warfare integrator (NWI) officer community. Overall, the
research team estimated the impact of streamlining organizations,
integration of emerging technologies, outsourcing work, and shifting
functions to the senior enlisted force. The dynamic factors and
influences will result in a smaller, more skilled, experienced (senior),
and joint officer corps.

A Look to the Future

This research identifies elements that will cause changes in the size
and structure of the Navy's future officer force and assesses the ability of the Navy's personnel structure to accommodate such changes.
Dynamic elements that will create or affect changes in the personnel
structure have been addressed in many documents. *Joint Vision
2010* envisioned that, as we move toward 2010, the dynamic changes
in our security environment would include potential adversaries,
technological advances, information superiority, enhanced joint-

ness, and multinational operations.[2] The Navy's ability to adapt its force to keep pace with these changes will determine how well it can perform its mission in 2010.

Joint Vision 2020 addresses the need to make full use of the increasingly capable information technology and indicates that Information Operations may evolve into a separate mission area requiring the services to maintain appropriately designed organizations and trained specialists.[3] The Navy's current efforts to keep up with information technology changes include the creation of a specialized career track for the information professional (IP).[4] The pace of technological change is expected to continue and even accelerate, creating demand for increased reliance on technology and for experts who can use it to the best advantage.

Causes for Change in the Naval Officer Structure

This study assessed the potential changes that may occur in the future naval officer force. The following categories explain the major causes for change in the officer force. These dynamic factors categorize personnel changes and were derived from a blend of government reports and previous RAND studies. They are useful to assess potential future changes to the naval officer force:

1. Force structure changes are increases or decreases to the force structure (e.g., changes in the number of units, aircraft, ships, logistic elements, and operational staffs).

2. Structure/doctrinal/organizational structure changes include manpower changes as a result of organizational structure

---

[2]Joint Chiefs of Staff, *Joint Vision 2010*, p. 8.

[3]Joint Chiefs of Staff, *Joint Vision 2020,* p. 36.

[4]NAVADMIN 182/01 CNO WASHINGTON DC R 251530Z JUL 01 Subject: Establishment of Information Professional and Human Resources Officer Communities and Fleet Support Officer (FSO) Transition. The IP community will provide expertise in information, command and control, and space systems through the planning, acquisition, operation, maintenance, and security of systems that support Navy operational and business processes. It will provide specialized officers in the information and space technologies that are the building blocks of the command, control, communications, and computer architecture, as well as the information and knowledge elements essential for knowledge superiority.

changes, alignment/realignment, and changes to existing structure or doctrine causing unit adjustment (e.g., aircraft/ship/weapon system changes, unit reconfigurations, program element transfers).

3. Wartime shortages refer to increases to address valid manning shortages (e.g., increases to meet the authorized level of organization shortfalls), including manpower changes occurring as a result of emerging threats and missions.

4. Emerging technologies include manpower changes derived from evolving scientific and technical advances (e.g., research and development advances), and data processing improvements. This category includes manpower reductions resulting from efficiencies gained through technological breakthroughs and improvements such as increased automation in engineering plants and damage control systems and improvements to ship control and navigation functions.

5. Changed functional requirements are modifications/changes in functional areas as a result of adjusted workload or methods of operation (e.g., manpower standards, staffing guides, crew ratios). Functional requirement changes are considered to be those resulting from innovation such as initiatives developed using "Smart Ship" technology, to include reduced watch-standers, all enlisted bridge watch teams, and cross-training of crewmembers in order to minimize manpower requirements for watch-standing. On the support side, BRAC, as well as outsourcing and privatization of officer billets, is included in this category of change.

6. Increases or decreases to joint activities may also be a source of officer growth or decline of manpower in the future. It is likely that joint activities and requirements may increase, as well as manpower requirements that directly support joint activities.

7. Increases or decreases will also occur in the training and transient personnel accounts. These changes are related to revisions in service training needs; in addition to changes to various individual accounts (e.g., student and instructor changes with service training directly related to force structure expansion or contraction). Changes may also result due to increases in the training bases to respond to emerging threats and missions.

While changes to the force structure and organizational structure will be described explicitly below, other causes for change outlined above will be accounted for within the discussion of officer communities affected. The causes of change to the officer force in 2010 will be different from the causes for change in 2017, and will be emphasized in the two scenarios.

THE NAVY FUTURE OFFICER FORCE, 2010

The 2000 to 2010 scenario is one of general stability and was built as a demand-based scenario. As the number and type of ships, submarines, and aircraft change as a result of commissioning and decommissioning, the number and specialties (designators) of officers who man them will correspondingly change. Nonetheless, force structure changes, organizational alignment, and the early stages of capitalizing on innovations as well as the introduction of new technologies each influence 2010 future officer manpower requirements with different effects by community. Future support forces are also anticipated to shrink as a result of BRAC, outsourcing, and privatization. Therefore, as a result of these influences and effects, it is estimated that an overall slight decline in officer manpower over the 10-year period will occur, with approximately a 900-billet decrease in the unrestricted line officer community. Marginal changes are expected to occur within the staff, restricted line, and LDO/CWO communities. This officer manpower scenario allows analysis as to whether current officer management policies and practices are capable of developing and maintaining a desired inventory in a nominally steady-state environment.

Table 6.1 shows the degree to which different factors cause manpower numbers to change. (We have aggregated operational and support changes into a community view.) The two causes for change that affect almost all of the communities considered in the 2010 scenario are force structure changes and organizational structure changes. These two factors are discussed below in more detail and are followed by an explanation of resulting changes for each community.

Table 6.1

Summary of Changes to Naval Officer Manpower, 2000–2010

	AIR	SWO	SUB	SPEC-WAR	STAFF	RL	LDO/CWO
Force structure			– – –	+ +	– –	+ +	– – –
Organizational structure/ doctrine changes	– –	–	– –	+	– –		
Wartime shortages				+ + +		+ +	
Emerging technologies		– –				+ + +	+ +
Changed functional requirements	– – –	– – –			– –		+
Joint/defense activities				+		+ +	
Training/ transient				+			
Other				+			

+ = increase in manpower, *little* impact.

+ + = increase in manpower, *moderate* impact.

+ + + = increase in manpower, *most* impact.

– = decrease in manpower, *little* impact.

– – = decrease in manpower, *moderate* impact.

– – – = decrease in manpower, *most* impact.

Force Structure Changes

The estimated impact of force structure changes from 2000 to 2010 was determined by adding or subtracting the officer manning for each unit or class of ship or submarine as it is planned to be placed into or taken out of commission. As a new ship was commissioned, the manning associated with that platform was added to the "operational forces" future requirement. Similarly, as a unit was decommissioned, the manning for that class of ship decreased the future requirement. Unit officer manning was determined by "pulling" the number of officers by grade and designator by the UIC against the manning reflected for that unit in the database, and adding or subtracting this manning as ships, submarines, or aircraft carriers are placed into or out of commission. Table 6.2 details the expected changes in platforms between 2000 and 2010. Although the number of platforms in the fleet will be roughly the same during this period, new platforms entering the fleet will incorporate emerging technology enhancements, such as increased automation in engineering plants, improvements in damage control capabilities, ship control upgrades, reduced maintenance in deck coatings, and innovations being developed and tested in Smart Ship fleet experiments, which include reduced watch-standing requirements.

There are several new ship classes for which manning profiles have not been published in open sources, and assumptions were made regarding the number of officers manning those platforms. The assumptions are as follows: LPD-17 is assumed to be manned quantitatively and qualitatively as the LPD-4; the DD(X) is assumed to have the same officer structure as the DDG-51; and *Virginia*-class submarines are assumed to have the same officer complement as the *Los Angeles*–class submarines. These are considered to be conservative assumptions, as there is a trend toward reducing the number of personnel aboard vessels at sea.

Organizational Structure Changes

The Atlantic and Pacific Fleet combatant commanders each has five subordinate "type" commanders who oversee specific categories of

Table 6.2

Expected Changes in Platforms Between 2000 and 2010

Platforms	POR 2000	Leaving the Fleet	Joining the Fleet	POR 2010
Carriers	12	2	2	12
Surface combatants	116	34	34	116
Submarines	74	16	6	64
Amphibious ships	39	16	13	36
Combat logistics force	34	17	12	29
Support	21	0	0	21
Mine warfare	15	0	0	15
Command ships	5	3	3	5
Aircraft	2,555	various	various	2,547

SOURCE: Program of Record (POR), U.S. Navy.

forces and activities: Naval Air Force, Naval Surface Force, Submarine Force, Training Command, and a Naval Construction Brigade. The Commander, Naval Reserve Force commands the Naval Reserve through two lower-echelon commands, the Naval Air Reserve and Naval Surface Reserve forces. Type commanders (TYCOMs) primarily supervise personnel, training, logistics, maintenance, and other support to ships, aircraft, and units.

Recent alignment actions have been taken as the Chief of Naval Operations (CNO) assigned the U.S. Atlantic Fleet combatant commander with additional duties and title of "U.S. Fleet Forces Command," which will provide him with a bigger voice in developing the ways that ships and crews are trained and prepared for deployment.[5] This assignment followed similar changes the CNO made in which he designated lead/follow relationships among the surface warfare, aviation, and submarine TYCOMs. The lead TYCOMs will now report to U.S. Fleet Forces Command to advise on modernization requirements and training issues. The goal of this alignment is to build common Navy-wide policies between fleets and to eliminate any differences in the way the force is trained.[6]

We posit that further streamlining actions will be taken by 2010 to align command structures. Commands that are anticipated to be realigned include TYCOMs. Efficiencies will be gained by merging the Atlantic and Pacific TYCOM staffs into a single TYCOM staff; for example, Surface Forces, Atlantic, and Surface Forces, Pacific, will merge into one command—under Commander, Naval Surface Forces. The same is projected to occur for Naval Air Forces and Naval Submarine Forces. Merging these staffs will result in streamlining command structures and reducing parallel functions to include administrative, operations and scheduling, logistics, and development of training requirements. However, elements within each TYCOM are responsible for training the crews of aircraft, ships, and submarines, and the numbers of these billets would not be changed in a realignment effort. The headquarters elements of each TYCOM will be combined, but liaison elements will remain within each geographic region as necessary. The merging of TYCOMs will

[5]Eisman (2001).
[6]Carl (2001).

continue the progress toward the goal of alignment and will capital-ize on the ability to communicate instantly, taking advantage of developing technologies that will provide worldwide visibility of per-sonnel and logistics assets. Further, a streamlined and centralized command structure reinforces the establishment of plans and poli-cies leading to a common baseline of training within the Atlantic and Pacific Fleets. Merging TYCOMs is assessed to result in a 25 percent reduction, at the O-4 to O-6 levels, in the TYCOM headquarters staff. The 2010 scenario incorporates these reductions.

On the support forces side, several factors will affect "shore support" officer manning. The right-sizing of support forces will include con-ducting another round of BRAC to bring support forces in line with the decreases that have occurred during the downsizing to the "operational" forces. In addition, further pressure will exist to create "shore support" savings by shifting jobs from military personnel to civilians. A GAO review of support officer positions indicated that many naval officer positions ashore are candidates for military-to-civilian conversion.[7] Future efforts toward right-sizing the force will evaluate shore manning, as well as the need for naval officers in shore support positions. Change in naval officer positions is expected, and this will occur by the transfer of responsibilities from naval officers to either civil service employees, other civilians through outsourcing and privatization, or to the enlisted force. We recognize that in the current decentralized shore manpower process, claimants themselves will need to effect these officer manpower changes.

Changes in Unrestricted Line Officer Manpower

SWO manning in operational forces—forces assigned primarily to sea or those that directly support sea-going forces—has steadily decreased over the past decade. This decrease follows the overall downsizing trend in the 1990s. Recent SWO "operational forces" manning trends indicate that downsizing continued through 1998 and leveled off in 1999 and 2000. From 1990 to 2000, SWO "operational forces" decreased by approximately 38 percent. In view

---

[7]GAO (1996).

of the significant decrease during the drawdown period, it is anticipated that SWO decreases through 2010 will occur more slowly. Current force structure and future shipbuilding plans reflected in the Program of Record (POR), and Carrier Battle Group (CVBG) presence requirements established in the Global Naval Force Presence Policy (GNFPP) indicate a steady demand for ships and the SWOs who man them. Although there is pressure to reduce at-sea manning, only marginal changes to SWO manning are anticipated to occur from 2000 to 2010.

Overall, the trend has been downward, and it is assumed that there will be some continued pressure to reduce and optimize manning at sea.[8] Pressure to streamline "operational forces" at sea is anticipated to reduce the officer structure, primarily at the junior officer level. An estimated 5 percent reduction of SWO officers in the O-1 and O-2 paygrades will occur between 2000 and 2010.

Across all paygrades, the forecasted net change to SWO authorizations between 2000 and 2010 is a decrease of approximately 350 officers. These reductions are attributed to several factors. The major effect will be the result of changes to force structure and changed functional requirements resulting from Smart Ship innovations, including reduced watch-standers, minimized watch teams, and cross-training of crewmembers to minimize manpower requirements for watch-standing. Emerging technology will result in efficiencies gained from automation in engineering plants and damage-control systems. In addition, improvements to ship control and navigation functions will also reduce SWO officer requirements. Finally, TYCOM realignment will marginally reduce SWO headquarters manning requirements ashore. On the support side, BRAC and the outsourcing and privatization of officer billets will also contribute to reducing SWO authorizations.

---

[8]A 1999 Office of Naval Research study reviewed efforts to optimize manning on naval ships. The study indicated that although the Navy's total budget declined by 40 percent since 1985, operations and support (O&S) costs have remained almost constant. Because personnel costs make up over 50 percent of O&S costs, reducing the number of people necessary to man ships of the future as well as the legacy ships of today's fleet is considered essential to reducing O&S funds to recapitalize and modernize the fleet. See NRAC (2000b).

Submarine officer operational manning also decreased during the 1990s. From 1990 to 2000, submarine officer operational authorizations fell by approximately 37 percent. Planned future force structure changes will cause further decreases in operational submarine officer manning, and the effect of force structure changes appears significant. Overall, between 2000 and 2010, submarine officer manning will be reduced by approximately 400 officers. This number reflects force structure changes that occur as a result of reduction in submarines and the merging of Atlantic and Pacific submarine TYCOMs.

Aviation officer operational authorizations decreased approximately 30 percent from 1990 to 1995. Since 1995, aviation operational force manning has remained relatively stable. Looking to the future, the changes in the number of aircraft contained in the POR force structure from 2000 to 2010 are minimal, and therefore little change from that factor is anticipated to occur in aviation officer manning.[9] The major impact to aviation manning through 2010 is anticipated to result from changed functional requirements, that is, primarily occurring from reductions in shore support officer billets as a result of outsourcing and privatization. Merging of TYCOMs will yield only minor changes in the aviation officer structure. In total, only marginal changes are expected to occur in 2000–2010 in the aviation community.

The remaining unrestricted line officer communities are the fleet support officers (FSOs), SWOs, and special operations officers. In October 2001, FSOs will transition into the newly created human resources (HR) and IP communities, some will laterally transfer to the supply community, and a relatively small number will remain within the FSO community. It is assumed that by 2010, FSOs will no longer be in the officer inventory, as the remaining FSOs will have been either retired or redesignated. Because a majority of FSOs will transfer from the unrestricted line to the restricted line communities of HR and IP as well as the supply community, this will result in a decrease of unrestricted line officers and an increase in restricted line officers.

---

[9]The POR force structure is provided in Appendix B.

Trend analysis indicates that special warfare officers have decreased since 1995. However, the demand for officer manning of the special warfare community is anticipated to increase. Emerging missions and existing asymmetrical threats will lead to increased missions and taskings for these forces. Given their unique capabilities and con-sidering that the special warfare community is small, emerging threats and missions will cause an increase in force structure for this community. Additionally, increases are expected to result from unit reconfiguration to meet asymmetrical threats as well as to support Joint Forces. This small community is predicted to grow by 15 per-cent between now and 2010.

Special operations officers include explosive ordnance disposal (EOD) and mine countermeasures (MCM) officers, and the com-munity has a small number of officers (approximately 350). The outlook for special operations officers is that, as a result of a recent Surface Warfare Commander's Conference decision, it will shift from a community with four specialties to a single warfare specialty. This shift will include a transfer of functions previously performed by EOD community officers to other communities. For example, SWOs will begin to command rescue and salvage ships. The focus of the EOD community will shift to the warfighting requirements of EOD, underwater MCM, and leadership in mobile diving and salvage. The assessment is that there will be an increased demand for special operations officers to accommodate support of counterterrorism and force protection measures, and thus a slight upward trend in manning is expected.

Changes in Restricted Line Officer Manpower

The restricted line includes engineering duty officers, aerospace engineering duty officers, cryptologic officers, intelligence officers, public affairs officers, and oceanographers—equating to roughly 8 percent of the Navy. There is virtually no change to the restricted line as a result of force structure and TYCOM reorganization changes. However, the restricted line population increases as a result of the creation of HR and IP designators and the transfer of FSOs from the unrestricted line to those designators within the restricted line community.[10] The HR community is made up of converted FSOs, while the IP community is populated with existing lieutenant through captain (O-3 to O-6) space and electronic warfare officers, as well as converted FSOs. In addition, it is anticipated that future demand will increase the need for intelligence and cryptologic officers. Intelligence officer operational manning has increased modestly since 1993, and this trend is expected to continue. The same assessment applies for cryptologic officers, as their expertise is necessary in understanding and forming responses to emerging threats. Extending the recent OPA trend of 1995–2000 to 2010 indicates a modest increase in restricted line officers.

Changes in Staff Corps Manpower

Officers in the medical, Judge Advocate General (JAG), supply, chaplain, and Civil Engineer Corps (CEC) communities populate the Staff Corps. The future assessment for the Staff Corps officer manning is that a relatively stable Staff Corps is anticipated from 2000 to 2010, with only marginal reductions anticipated. Medical, JAG, chaplain, and CEC officers will remain at relatively the same manning levels as in 2000, while Supply Corps officer manning is projected to decrease by approximately 250 officers from 2000 to 2010. This decrease occurs as the result of force structure reduction, organizational alignment, and outsourcing and civilianizing of supply shore establishment officer requirements.

Changes in Limited Duty Officer Manpower

LDOs are assigned to 32 designators in the surface warfare, submarine, and aviation communities, as well as the general series and Staff Corps. Projected force structure changes for 2010 will have a varied effect on different LDO designators. The need for some LDO technicians will decrease relatively more than others, a few will remain unchanged, and some will have increased requirements. However, the net result of force structure and TYCOM reorganization to the LDO community is negligible. The recent trend in LDO operational force

---

[10]The HR and IP restricted line designators were formally established on October 1, 2001.

manning has been a gradual increase since 1996, indicating an increasing need for their unique experience and expertise. It is anticipated that this trend will continue through 2010.

Changes in Chief Warrant Officer Manpower

The CWO population includes surface warfare, submarine, aviation, general, supply, and civil engineering officers who fill 31 different designators. Like LDOs, CWOs are technical experts. CWO operational manning has decreased since 1988, but the number of CWO authorizations leveled off in 1999 and 2000. Looking to 2010, the impact of force structure changes and TYCOM reorganization on the CWO community is assessed to be minimal. The trend in OPA from 2000 to 2005 also indicates a gradual decrease for CWOs. Given the consistent decrease of CWO authorizations, continued minor reductions through 2010 are expected.

We forecast small increases for LDOs and small decreases for CWOs based on recent trends, with a small increase overall for the two combined. None of the separate factors we apply (see Table 6.1) changes this assessment. The LDO and CWO communities are the only communities in which factors cause change in opposite directions. Moreover, the similarities of these two communities (technical experts) might lead to merging one into the other but in overall numbers would not change significantly.

2000–2010 Summary

The 2010 scenario employs marginal changes to refine the officer force, given knowledge and assumptions about force structure and organizational change, as well as other causes for change. While these factors affect almost all communities, the effects vary. In general, the surface warfare, submarine, and aviation communities, as well as the Staff Corps, face small decreases in their authorizations, while the special warfare community increases in response to mission needs, and the restricted line will increase largely as a result of administrative changes. LDOs are increasingly valued for their technical expertise and enjoy a modest increase overall, while CWOs experience a slight decline. The quantitative result of these changes is presented and compared with the 2017 scenario at the conclusion of this chapter.

THE NAVY FUTURE OFFICER FORCE, 2017

Transformation is currently a much discussed topic within defense and Navy circles. There is wide recognition that while the need for transformation is immediately apparent, there is a small likelihood that actual transformation will be particularly rapid. In part, the progress of transformation for the Navy is constrained by its legacy ships, submarines, aircraft, weapons, and systems. As potential enemy capabilities are evaluated and the Navy transforms accordingly, the peacetime process will evolve at a pace commensurate with the cost-effective utilization of legacy systems. Thus, the Navy of 2017 will include significant numbers of ships, submarines, and aircraft that are currently under construction or in the fleet today. The manpower required to support those legacy systems will, in all likelihood, closely resemble today's manpower with a few small exceptions. Those exceptions (to legacy-systems manpower) will reflect the incremental effects of long-term trends predictable in nature but unpredictable in specifics.

Table 6.3 summarizes the factors that will shape the 2017 officer structure. The long-term trends that affect manpower will include force structure reductions, an increase in the need for both general and integrative experience in the unrestricted line, and an increased need for specific experience within the restricted line and among LDOs and CWOs. The major causes for change for officer personnel requirements between 2010 and 2017 are posited to be attributable to force structure changes, organizational alignment, and decreases in the shore establishment through changed functional requirements via outsourcing and privatization. These forces affecting future changes in manpower are rooted in budget pressures, need for cost effectiveness, or the need for technology improvements and enhancements. The net effect on both enlisted personnel and officers will be fewer personnel, increased seniority, an older but still vigorous force, and more integration and specialization. The specialization will play out in the restricted line and LDO/CWO communities. The need for greater integration across unrestricted line

Table 6.3

Summary of Changes to Naval Officer Manpower, 2010–2017

	AIR	SWO	SUB	SPEC-WAR	STAFF	RL	LDO/CWO
Force structure	− − −	− − −	− − −		− −	− −	+
Organizational structure/ doctrine changes	− −	− −	− −	+ + +	− − −		
Wartime shortages							
Emerging technologies	−	−	−	+ +		+ + +	+ + +
Changed functional requirements	− −	− −	− −	+ +	−	+ + +	+ + +
Joint/defense activities				+			
Training/ transient				+			
Other							

+ = increase in manpower, *little* impact.
+ + = increase in manpower, *moderate* impact.
+ + + = increase in manpower, *most* impact.
− = decrease in manpower, *little* impact.
− − = decrease in manpower, *moderate* impact.
− − − = decrease in manpower, *most* impact.

communities and with other services is the impetus for a new community of O-5 and O-6 unrestricted line officers, which we have labeled naval warfare integrators. The NWI community emerges to accommodate the need for experienced warfare officers with a broad view across forces, platforms, systems, weapons, and sensors.

Overall Impact

The factors affecting naval officer manpower for 2017 include changes to force structure (numbers of ships, aircraft, submarines, and units), organizational structure (includes streamlining of command and control elements), functional requirements (increases or decreases in the size of crews and staffing because of adjusted operating methods), and the use of emerging technologies. These factors are inextricably linked, and their dynamic and combined effect will change future officer requirements; for example, emerging technology has resulted in more capable surface warfare combatants, fewer crew staffing requirements, and a reduced force structure. These factors combine to increase or decrease manpower, and their effects vary by community.

The number of officers required will probably decrease as other types of manpower are chosen for cost-efficiency reasons. Thus efforts to civilianize, to convert from active to reserve, to contract out, and to change from officer to enlisted requirements will continue. While much attention has focused on optimizing manning and reducing life-cycle costs of ships at sea, a similar focus is needed to optimize manning ashore. A GAO study criticized the way the Navy establishes shore officer requirements.[11] Hence, increased attention in streamlining shore officer requirements will result in the Navy gaining efficiencies in manning shore establishments from 2010 to 2017. Through outsourcing and privatization, support forces will decrease. Conversely, the movement of traditional officer functions to the enlisted ranks is anticipated because of fundamental changes to Navy policies and practices. Examples of such functions include Officer of the Deck Underway and Engineering Officer of the Watch underway watches, which have traditionally been officer functions. With an increasingly more educated, skilled, and experienced enlisted force, a trend is anticipated toward more enlisted personnel assuming traditional officer roles and tasks. Generally, this officer-to-enlisted transfer of functions will pass from junior officers to senior enlisted personnel.

The increased utilization of LDOs (possibly merged with the CWO community) emerges as a practical and valuable alternative in the force of the future. Future equipment and systems will be more technically complex. Experienced operators who have been grown from the enlisted community can bridge the technology gap as systems evolve. Further, the retention patterns of LDOs can fill downturns in the retention of junior officers. As the junior officer Minimum Service Requirement expires, many junior officers leave active service. LDOs can bridge the gap as they do not have as steep a drop-

---

[11]GAO (1997).

off in retention as unrestricted line junior officers, and provide a stable, technically oriented experience base to meet future needs.[12]

The next sections address the four primary forces of change for 2017, followed by the impact of such change for each community.

Force Structure Transformation

The 2017 scenario is based on an assessment of the proportion of the inventory that will be legacy as compared with the proportion that might reflect transformation. Table 6.4 shows the force structure that exists in the year 2000 and the legacy structure that is projected for years 2010 and 2017. Using current and 2010 numbers from the POR, we estimate that at least 67 percent of a force structure of nominally today's size would be legacy systems. Conversely, no more than about 33 percent of today's or 2010's force structure would be transformed by 2017.

Table 6.4

Legacy Force Structure

Force Structure	2000 Baseline	2010 Legacy Force Structure	2017 Legacy Force Structure
Aircraft carriers	12	12	8
Aircraft	2,555	2,547	1,673
Ships	230	222	186
Submarines	74	64	43

[12]Conversations with Navy officials indicate that CWOs are considered interchangeable in the assignment process with LDOs up to the O-3 paygrade. At the lieutenant commander (O-4) level, LDOs occupy more senior leadership and management positions. As Navy ships, submarines, and aircraft systems and equipment become more complex, the need to retain the technical expertise that CWOs have acquired and can provide will become more apparent. However, compensation and promotion factors have resulted in CWO-3s experiencing an attrition rate of 23 percent per year. Establishing a greater pay differential between CWO-3s and CWO-4s, as well as the use of the W-5 paygrade may provide sufficient incentive to keep CWOs in the Navy and maximize their expert contributions.

As to the nature of the approximately 33 percent of the force structure that reflects transformation, we determined that, from a manpower perspective, significant reductions would occur in enlisted manpower, and lesser reductions in officer manpower even as some officer billets convert to enlisted. The trends in force structure are toward very lightly manned platforms, such as DD(X), or to unmanned platforms (e.g., unmanned aerial vehicles [UAVs]). Without determining specifics, we see that a recurring theme involves reductions in manpower in future systems because technology will be used to reduce manpower and maximize the use of unmanned assets to increase combat effectiveness while reducing potential for casualties, and also because savings from the manpower and personnel account (MPN) will be used for recapitalization and modernization.

New technologies in the force structure will noticeably reduce the number of enlisted personnel while having little effect on the number of officers required. For example, the Smart Ship Project Assessment recommended a decrease of approximately 50 personnel. Although some officer reductions were addressed as potential candidates for this reduction, the forwarded report only recommended enlisted reductions.[13]

Organizational Structure Changes

The future organizational structure of the Navy will continue to be refined. The CNO's vision for the future is that of an agile force; a fluid organizational command and control structure that is able to anticipate, counter, and defeat potential threats; and a structure networked at every level and integrated with the Allies.[14] The command and control organizational structure and headquarters elements needed to support future missions will be more streamlined than those of 2002. Emerging technology, instant communications, worldwide visibility of assets and resources, and a shared operational picture will produce efficiencies in command and control and administrative and logistics functions and will reduce staffing

---

[13]In the Smart Ship Project Assessment, COMNAVSURFLANT provided a list of recommended billet reductions to the CNO. Reference Enclosure (1) to COMNAVSURFLANT ltr 3980 Ser N6/1687 of September 19, 1997.

[14]Remarks of ADM Vern Clark, Current Strategy Forum, Newport, R.I., June 12, 2001.

requirements. Manning reductions in headquarters elements will result in a streamlined organizational structure from warfighters to the combatant commanders.

Emerging Technologies

Manpower reductions resulting from technological breakthroughs and improvements are expected to continue through 2017 and beyond. It is anticipated that future development and emerging technologies will focus on reducing overall life-cycle costs through reduced manpower requirements. Future ship designs will feature increased automation and integration with other units, resulting in reduced manpower requirements. UAVs will augment or replace some manned aircraft missions to a greater extent than they do today. Unmanned underwater vehicles will become a force multiplier to the submarine fleet, extending the reach and capability of onboard sensors and systems. Emerging technologies will decrease the manpower requirements of the surface warfare, aviation, and submarine communities. Anticipated effects on other communities are addressed below.

Changed Functional Requirements

By 2017, changes in functional areas resulting from adjusted methods of operation will have some impact on the unrestricted line officer community. Optimized manning at sea and increased use of unmanned platforms will reduce manpower standards (such as watch-standing and scheduled maintenance work), staffing, and crew ratios in future platforms. These changes will decrease manpower requirements in the aviation, surface warfare, and submarine communities. The staff community will also experience decreases in staffing requirements as a result of contracting, outsourcing, and privatization of functions normally conducted by staff officers ashore. The new community of NWIs (discussed in more detail below) will emerge. The use of LDOs will increase as a result of a greater need for specialists, rather than generalists, to maintain and operate more highly technical equipment and systems aboard future platforms.

Naval Warfare Integrators

By 2017, the Navy will be experiencing a major transformation in doctrine and process. Naval warfare will have moved away from combat, expressed in terms of the platforms employed, and moved toward warfighting, expressed in terms of sensors, connectivity, and the employment of diverse systems and weapons, all of which may be positioned on manned or unmanned platforms—beneath, on, or above the sea. Major shipbuilding programs between 2010 and 2017 have favored lightly or unmanned platforms. In 2017, although the numbers of ships and submarines are nominally equivalent to 2001 numbers, about one-third will use optimized manning.

In 2017, officers assigned to operational units must not only be proficient and knowledgeable of Navy systems and capabilities but also must possess a broad understanding of joint capabilities of units (and likely combined and interagency capabilities). Future operations will require an integrative approach to warfighting, using all services and theater assets. Future naval officers will have broader responsibilities to integrate off-ship sensors and weapons, and an officer with increased experience and specialization will be a necessary element for conducting future operations. To highlight the need for increased experience and specialization, we created a new designator reflective of the need for an officer with general skills and experience dictated by the factors that would transform the Navy. The Navy has had a growing need for naval officers skilled and experienced in the technologically sophisticated environment of 2017. By 2017, the accelerating pace of technological change will have transformed Navy connectivity with the establishment of information, sensor, and engagement grids. Under the Navy's network-centric warfare concept, surface warfare combatant and other naval warfare platforms will be seamlessly linked with each other, with other services' units, and with theater and national sensors in a real-time network.

Network-centric warfare has now become a reality, and the need now exists for senior operators, tacticians, and decisionmakers to exploit this technology to the Navy's best advantage. The demands of the systems, tactics, and strategies require much higher levels of knowledge and experience than had been required in the platform-specific 1990s. Thus, the future officer force must have people who are technically competent to integrate these many sources of information, knowledgeable of the capabilities of assets to counter these threats, and who occupy a position of authority sufficient to decide on weapon of choice, on- or off-platform, necessary to counter the threat. Thus, by 2017, we posit a plan to establish a new unrestricted line designator, NWI, for senior unrestricted line officers.

Senior experienced officers will be knowledgeable of this shared system of sensors and weapons and be in position to make decisions about employing them in the future Navy's integrated and cooperative approach to warfighting. Senior warfighters—NWIs—will gain the working knowledge of warfare communities' and other services' systems and capabilities through warfare-specific experience tours, NWI training in service, command pipeline training, Joint Professional Military Education, and joint/combined/interagency assignments. The designation of senior (O-5 and O-6) unrestricted line "warfighters" as NWIs recognizes the connectivity that will be available among all future warfare communities and services.[15] The continued development of integrated capabilities and experienced officers who will use them will result in a more ready and capable Navy. The ability to integrate warfare community and service capabilities, and to make decisions regarding their use, will require a more capable, experienced, and joint officer corps.

Selection for the NWI designator will first be determined at the O-5 (commander) selection board. Recognizing the need for senior officers to be proficient in network-centric warfare and information technologies, one-half of all unrestricted line surface warfare,

---

[15]Under the Navy's network-centric warfare concept, surface warfare combatant and other naval warfare platforms will be seamlessly linked with each other and with theater and national sensors in a real-time network. One of the Navy's revolutionary technologies that will play a big role in making this possible, particularly for integrated theater air and missile defense, is called Cooperative Engagement Capability. Cooperative Engagement Capability processors automatically share fire control-quality targeting data for airborne threats in seconds among different surface warships and E-2C aircraft as well as Army and Marine Corps air defense systems ashore, allowing them to act as a single distributed defense system over a wide geographic area. Ships can use the data to engage targets without actually tracking them with their own sensors. Navy surface warfare officials consider Cooperative Engagement Capability perhaps the most important of all the planned upgrades to the Aegis ships. "[Cooperative Engagement Capability] represents not just how the Navy will operate and fight," ADM Michael Mullen told *Armed Forces Journal International* (Goodman, 1999, p. 44), "but how the services will operate and fight. It is a cornerstone for that future."

submarine, and aviation officers selected to O-5 will be designated as NWIs. Further, upon selection to O-6 (captain), all unrestricted line surface warfare, submarine, and aviation officers will be designated as NWIs. The goal is to select and nurture a core of officers trained in the integrated battlefield and fully conversant in effects-based transplatform capabilities.[16]

Changes in Unrestricted Line Officer Manpower

Our assessment of officer requirements for 2017 is that the numbers of officers in the unrestricted line surface warfare, submarine, and aviation operational forces decline as a result of force structure changes, changed functional requirements for manning platforms, further alignment to the organizational structure of operational forces, and through maximizing efficiencies gained by using innovative methods and emerging technologies. In addition, the number of officers in supporting forces falls by a figure commensurate with the most recent trends.[17]

To posit the unrestricted line surface warfare, submarine, and aviation officer profile from 2010 to 2017, the following method was used. In the aggregate, O-1 to O-6 paygrades were reduced by approximately 12 percent, which reflects force structure changes, changed functional manning requirements, emerging technology and innovation, and reduction of support forces.[18] Then, 50 percent of all O-5s were transferred to the NWI community, as detailed above. All O-6s are designated as NWIs.

Submarine and SWO requirements are posited to decrease between 2000 to 2010 as a result of force structure changes, organizational realignment, pressure to reduce manning and crew staffing requirements, and increased use of emerging technologies to support optimized manning. For the aviation community, only marginal

---

[16]Hagerott (2001). In this article, Commander Hagerott relates the need for the personnel system to build capability by making room for new knowledge areas and expertise of integrated/joint battlespace.

[17]Approximately 1.05 percent per year over the last three budgets.

[18]Support forces were reduced by approximately 7.6 percent, which is the cumulative trend of reductions taken over the last four budget years and applied to the seven-year period of 2010 to 2017.

changes are posited to occur between 2000 and 2010. However, between 2010 and 2017, the advent of the NWI community will have a major effect on the submarine, surface warfare, and aviation communities. As previously stated, 50 percent of submarine, SWO, and aviator O-5s will be redesignated as NWIs, and O-6 officers in these three communities will be redesignated as NWIs as well. Therefore, with the addition of half of the O-5s and 100 percent of O-6 submarine, surface warfare, and aviation officers, NWIs have had the greatest relative increase in the officer community. In 2017, the NWI community will be populated with approximately 2,600 O-5 and O-6 unrestricted line officers.

The special warfare community is posited to have an increase in requirements from 2000 to 2010 as a result of emerging threats and missions. From 2010 to 2017, special warfare manning levels will be maintained relatively stable at the 2010 levels. Requirements for special operations officers are expected to gradually decrease from 2010 to 2017.

Figure 6.2 illustrates the effects of dynamic changes to the officer force. FY 2000 is the base year of officer requirements, and thus is generally positioned at 100 percent, with the exception of NWI, which did not exist at that time. The percentages indicated for charted values for 2010 are percentages of requirements in relation to the FY 2000 value, and the charted percentage values for 2017 are in relation to the 2010 values. The most dramatic changes are those to the surface warfare, submarine, and aviation communities, given the introduction of the NWI community. FSOs began transitioning to HR, IP, and supply communities in October 2001. By 2010, all FSOs will have been either redesignated or retired from active service.

Changes in Restricted Line Officer Manpower

Overall, restricted line officer manning is posited to remain relative stable from 2000 to 2017 (see Figure 6.3). As equipment becomes more complex through technological advances, an increasingly more specialized and educated force will be required to maintain and manage it. Engineering duty officers are specialists in areas of engineering, combat systems and command, control, communications,

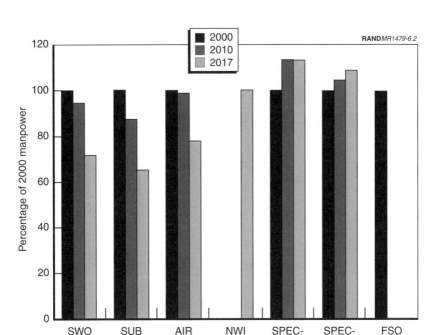

Figure 6.2—Expected Changes to Unrestricted Line Communities, 2000–2017

computers, and intelligence (C4I). Aerospace engineering duty officers are involved in the entire life cycle of aircraft, weapon, and naval space systems—from conception, to development and throughout the system's service. The need for these expert technicians will continue, and the pace at which emerging technologies advance within each of these areas requires a stable future officer force.

Likewise, cryptologic officers provide cryptologic and electronic warfare support to deployed ships, submarines, and aircraft; Signals Intelligence (SIGINT); and information warfare to minimize foreign exploitation of the Navy's electromagnetic system. Naval intelligence officers provide tactical, operational, and strategic intelligence support to naval forces, joint services, multinational forces, and decisionmakers. Emerging threats and missions will dictate the continued reliance on cryptologic and intelligence officers, and a stable

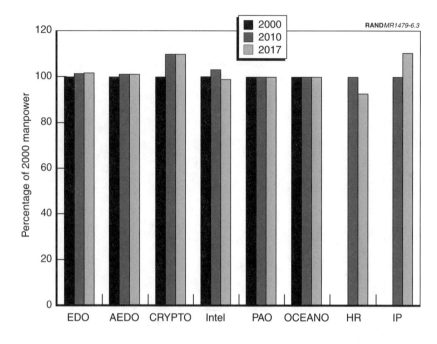

Figure 6.3—Expected Changes to Restricted Line Communities, 2000–2017

manning profile through the 2000–2017 period is anticipated. Future officer requirements for public affairs officers and oceanographers are posited to remain at 2000 levels. The HR designator was initiated in October 2001 and future requirements for HR officers will be reduced in line with reductions of shore activities. IPs also came into existence in October 2001. Rapid developments in information technology and the requirement to use this information through a connected network of shared sensors to engage a target will require a close connection of IP officers with the unrestricted line NWI community. We posit the IP community will grow, as the need for its expertise in information and command and control systems will be in greater demand as new technologies and capabilities expand and accelerate. Thus, 2017 will see greater demand for both specialists (e.g., IP) and generalists (e.g., NWI).

Changes in Staff Corps Manpower

Figure 6.4 illustrates the expected changes in the staff communities between 2000 and 2017. Medical community officer requirements will remain relatively stable through 2010.[19] However, as costs of maintaining a large medical "support" staff continue to rise, and as downward pressure acts on the operational forces, pressure for manpower and cost efficiencies will increase on the medical community, which may result in outsourcing and privatization efforts. As a result, the medical community is expected to see a decline in officer requirements between 2010 and 2017.

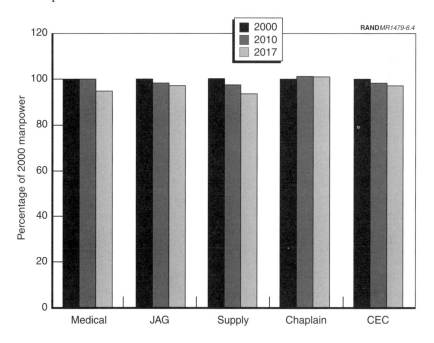

Figure 6.4—Expected Changes to Staff Communities, 2000–2017

---

[19]Marginal changes are posited to occur within the medical community between FY 2000 and FY 2010. Legislation related to TRICARE for Life, changed demographics of the military force—i.e., more servicemembers are married with spouses and family members entitled to and receiving military health care—and legislative changes will maintain the medical community at its present levels.

The requirement for JAG officers is expected to gradually decrease in this period. This decrease will result from a decrease in force structure and a resultant decrease in JAG officers required to support the requirement. Supply officers will also gradually decrease by approximately 250 officers from 2000 to 2010, as previously addressed. These decreases are the result of force structure reductions, organizational alignment, and the outsourcing of shore supply officer manning during this period. Continued decreases ashore are anticipated to occur from 2010 to 2017 for supply officers through outsourcing and privatization of shore supply officer duties. The Navy Chaplain Officer Corps is a small community, and only small changes in officer requirements are posited to occur between 2000 and 2017. CEC officers are primarily shore-based and likely to be gradually reduced in numbers between 2000 and 2017 in line with shore establishment decreases. This reduction will be the result of future base realignment and closures as well as privatization and outsourcing for their services.

Changes in Limited Duty Officer and Chief Warrant Officer Manpower

Emerging technologies will increase the need for LDO and CWO technical expertise. Technological advances will present the need for systems maintenance and operations experts, which LDOs and CWOs provide. In addition, as modifications are made to crew staffing requirements as the result of Smart Ship manning innovations and assessments, the demand for leaders with systems and equipment expertise will increase. Thus, as shown in Figure 6.5, the need for LDOs and CWOs will grow between 2000 and 2017.

2010–2017 Summary

Assuming a peacetime scenario,[20] the long-term forces affecting the officer corps will result in a smaller, more skillful, more senior and

---

[20]In the event of war, there may be increases in the size of the officer corps (as well as the numbers of enlisted personnel). However, as soon as the nation returns to a peacetime scenario, the long-term trend will come into play, albeit on a different, assumedly higher baseline.

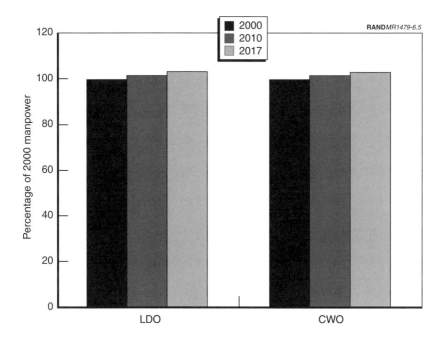

**Figure 6.5—Expected Changes to Limited Duty Officers and
Chief Warrant Officers, 2000–2017**

experienced, more specialized, and more joint officer corps. The new NWI designator moves officers from being platform "drivers" to being integrators of sensors, networks, and weapon systems, and the Navy overall becomes more integrated through the capabilities inherent in network-centric warfare. Existing and future platforms capitalize on technology and innovative concepts. Future platforms have the added advantage of a greater availability of shared sensors and weapon systems. Manning and managing units with such increased capability require officers schooled in integrated tactics.

In general, unrestricted line officers continue to be in demand, and a new community emerges to satisfy the need for broad warfare expertise. Staff officers ashore decrease in numbers as outsourcing and privatization occurs, and the demand for restricted line specialists remains relatively constant, even as some more technical communities increase in size. It is also anticipated that the demand for the unique talents of LDOs and CWOs will result in increases to those communities.

OFFICER MANAGEMENT IMPLICATIONS OF FUTURE MANPOWER REQUIREMENTS

The future scenarios described in the previous chapter posit possible manpower requirements for the Navy of 2010 and 2017. These scenarios are intended to test the flexibility of the existing management tools and to explore any policy changes required to respond to such changed requirements. Such analytical exercises can explore the transitional issues and steady-state tradeoffs. This chapter explores the transitional aspects of the surface warfare community as an example and then discusses the steady-state tradeoffs and management decisions necessary to satisfy the requirements as predicted for selected communities. While the future manpower scenarios are only posited, the policy tradeoffs elicited from this exercise apply to any manpower structure. In other words, regardless of whether a community needs to promote to O-4 a year early to meet requirements, earlier promotions will consistently mean that fewer individuals are promoted to that grade.

TRANSITION VERSUS STEADY-STATE: MANAGING THE SURFACE WARFARE COMMUNITY, 2010

This analysis considers officers as members of specific year group cohorts to posit how officers move through their careers and thus how officer management structures will look in the future. Figure 7.1 charts this format. Along the x-axis are years of commissioned service. The line on this figure indicates the current inventory of SWOs. The bars represent how the current authorizations for SWOs would look if they were divided, proportionately with the year groups

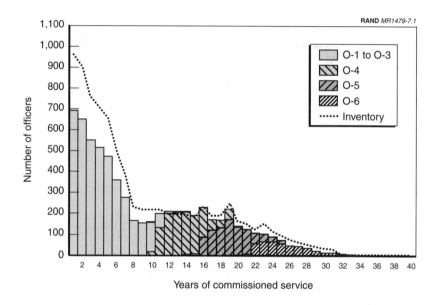

Figure 7.1—Current Surface Warfare Authorizations and Inventory,
by Year Group

of the current inventory, into year groups. The most junior group of officers include O-1s to O-3s with O-4s to O-6s shown with distinct shading. The delta between the line and the bars indicates that, as discussed in the previous chapters, there is currently an excess of junior SWOs compared with the authorizations for them.

Transitional Analysis

Transitional analysis suggests that if the current set of authorizations for SWOs remains constant, the surface warfare community can likely resolve the gaps, given current continuation rates and promotion opportunities. By transitional analysis, we mean that we project the current year group inventory forward over a time period to see the results. Thus, because there is a current excess of junior grade officers, as was evident in Figure 7.1, the surface warfare community will likely be able to satisfy the requirements in 2010, given that continuation behavior remains relatively similar to the current rates.

Figure 7.2 shows the shape of the surface warfare community, if accessions were decreased to satisfy the fewer requirements for junior officers. The "bump" at O-4 is a result of today's junior officers being promoted through the system. The darkened bars preceding each of the more senior grades represent the officers newly promoted to that grade and thus indicate promotion timing. In other words, the colored bars indicate, roughly from the left, O-1s to O-3s in the first shaded area; newly promoted O-4s and the rest of the O-4s; newly promoted O-5s and other O-5s; and newly promoted O-6s and other O-6s. Put another way, at 11 years of commissioned service, most of the officers are O-4s who were promoted the previous year. A smaller group of officers at 11 years of service are newly promoted O-4s, and an even smaller group of officers with 11 years of service are O-3s. The promotion opportunities reflected in this depiction are approximately 60 percent to O-4, 75 percent to O-5, and 51 percent to O-6. However, as the large cohort in O-4 is

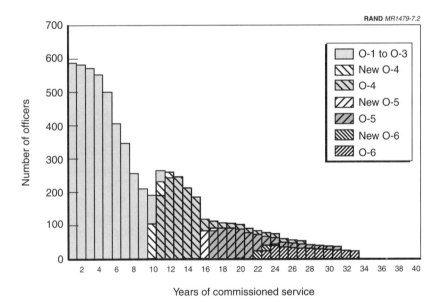

Figure 7.2—Surface Warfare Officers, 2010—As Current Junior Officers Progress Through System

promoted through this system, lower promotion opportunities to O-5 and O-6 will be necessary to reduce the overages at that grade. Further, once the large cohort leaves O-4, there will be a shortage of officers at that grade.

Steady-State Analysis

Rather than predicting the number of today's junior officers who will remain in the force to the year 2010 and shaping the force around them, another analytical approach is to examine the steady-state existence of the future force. The benefit of steady-state analysis is that it provides a target for policymakers, who prescribe the shape the force should take to meet future authorizations rather than placing them in the position, as above, of planning upon (or around) particularly large cohorts. Instead, steady-state analysis identifies, given the predicted requirements, what manpower policy will have to do to sustain such a force. One negative aspect of considering a steady-state system, of course, is that it assumes relatively little change in year-by-year requirements. We change requirements only twice (2010 and 2017 to coincide with the scenarios discussed earlier) and make two separate analyses given these changes to highlight policy tradeoffs for managing the force. We examine possible policy courses of action to meet the requirements. If these or similar choices are not made, the outcome will be gaps of the type previously discussed. The remainder of this chapter addresses the steady-state profiles of selected officer communities.

Figure 7.3 shows the steady-state inventory profile that matches the 2010 manpower scenario requirements for SWOs. This profile reflects slightly fewer accessions than today. The bars are less "jagged" in this chart (meaning that the bars either remain the same height or decrease in size as the years progress) because the entering year groups are all assumed to be the same size in the future, whereas Figures 7.1 and 7.2 reflected changes in sizes of accession year groups.

Some officers will continue to enter the surface warfare community from the aviation or submarine community, while the surface warfare community will also continue to supply warfare-qualified officers to other communities as well. To restrict the number of junior officers allowed in the system to the requirements and satisfy the need for O-4s, this career profile "fast tracks" a selected number of officers to O-4 with as early as seven years of service. This is a system that can adapt to the development needs of individuals and thus accommodate and reward those who demonstrate advanced capability and performance early. It is a person-based, not time-based, experience and development process. By fast-tracking and rewarding some officers, the actual number and percentage of O-3s promoted to O-4 decreases (to approximately 69 percent).[1] However, the percentage of officers promoted to O-5 increases (as high as 88 percent) as a result of this changed system, as fewer officers become O-4s and compete for promotion to O-5. Another change in this system is that longer careers are permitted for a small and selected number of O-5s. By keeping these officers as long as 31 years,[2] the Navy benefits from their experience and satisfies requirements for officers at this grade. Should these officers not be retained as long, the promotion rate to O-5 would have to increase to meet O-5 requirements (virtually all O-4s would be promoted). In such a system, however, the community would have additional difficulties satisfying O-4 requirements, as the parts of the system are always connected. A final difference between the proposed system and the current system is reflected in the promotion to O-6. Figure 7.3 indicates newly promoted O-6s appearing over eight years. By doing so, O-5s are encouraged to remain in the system because they

---

[1]The model calculates promotion results by including all officers promoted over time to that rank in the numerator, while using the number of officers that initially reach the zone as the denominator. For example, if there are 100 officers in a grade at year x, and 20 are promoted to the next grade in each year x+1, x+2, and x+3, then the total promotion opportunity to the next grade will be represented as 60 of 100 officers, or 60 percent. This is a different calculation from the current OSD model (as in Table 3.1), which takes the denominator from the in-zone year (equivalent to our x+2 in this example). Our models preclude calculating promotions the same as the current OSD calculations because of the longer promotion zones we employ. Thus, our promotion opportunity results are biased toward being lower and are not directly comparable to the current service calculations. Instead, they are relatively comparable with one another when exploring policy options and can also be compared to current service promotion results in Table 7.1 which are calculated using our formula.

[2]These models extend O-5s to 31 years of service and O-6s to 33 or 35 years of service (depending on the community). This tenure length was selected based on conversations with the research sponsor. Longer tenure could easily be modeled, although changes to it will result in changes to other model results, such as promotion timing and opportunity.

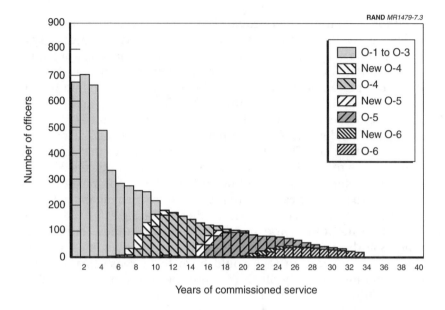

Figure 7.3—Surface Warfare Officers, 2010—In Steady-State

remain competitive, and more officers are eventually promoted to O-6. Changing promotion from a three-year zone to an eight-year zone increases the eventual promotion rate from 46 percent to 72 percent.

MANAGING THE SURFACE WARFARE COMMUNITY, 2017

The 2017 scenario for SWOs assumes further changes in require-ments, as was discussed in the prior chapter. Thus, the career system shown in Figure 7.4 indicates that accessions have dropped by another 100 officers, to slightly less than 600 officers per year. The management practices employed for 2017 are very similar to those of 2010. The primary difference in the career structures is the role of the NWI, which was introduced in the prior chapter. Fifty percent of SWOs will be transferred to the NWI community upon promotion to O-5. All SWOs promoted to O-6 will become NWIs. The resulting pattern of NWI officers is shown in Figure 7.5, which includes officers

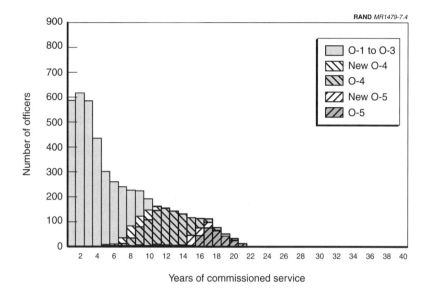

Figure 7.4—Surface Warfare Officers, 2017—In Steady-State

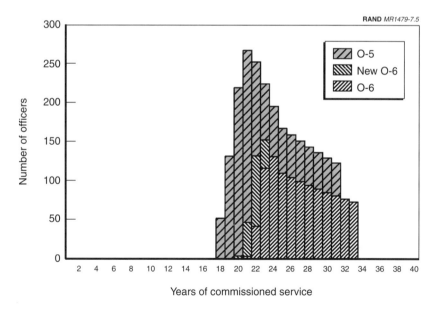

Figure 7.5—Naval Warfare Integrators, 2017—In Steady-State

originating from the surface warfare, submarine, and aviation communities. O-5 NWIs remain in the system as long as 31 years of service, and O-6s can remain in the service to 33 years.

MANAGING THE SUBMARINE COMMUNITY, 2010 AND 2017

The submarine community currently faces considerable management challenges, given the high proportion of O-4 requirements compared with those for more junior officers. As a result, the current inventory includes an excess of junior officers and O-5s compared with authorizations and a shortage of officers at O-4. The 2010 requirements include reductions at all grades for submariners, but, absent changes in management, the community will still suffer from shortages at O-4. Management changes are embodied in the steady-state representation of the community, shown in Figure 7.6. These modeling results indicate that some officers will need to be fast-tracked to O-4 in as early as nine years (two years earlier than the current system). The balance will be promoted at 10 years of service.

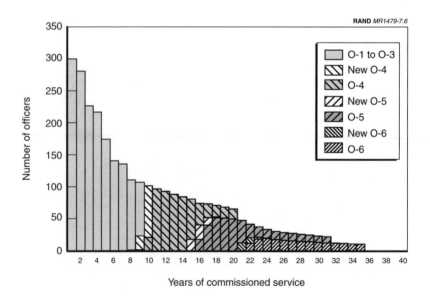

Figure 7.6—Submarine Officers, 2010—In Steady-State

These changes will require more flexible thinking about how officers are trained, assigned, and qualified for submarine warfare. Promotion to O-5 begins at 15 years of service (1 year earlier than current practice), but officers are promoted over a 3-year period to extend their time as O-4s and thus satisfy the requirements at that grade. A relatively small number of O-5s are permitted and provided incentives to stay in the Navy to 31 years of service. This additional six years beyond current practice helps to satisfy requirements at O-5, as the alternative would require more promotions to O-5 and thus would exacerbate O-4 shortages. Promotion to O-6 begins a year early at 21 years of service and a small number of O-6s are retained to 33 years (2 years beyond the current practice).

The submarine community is posited to decrease further by 2017. Figure 7.7 indicates that fewer accessions are necessary to meet the requirements of 2017. Otherwise, management practices remain similar to those discussed above for 2010, until such point in a career when the submarine officer is transferred to the NWI community, shown in Figure 7.5.

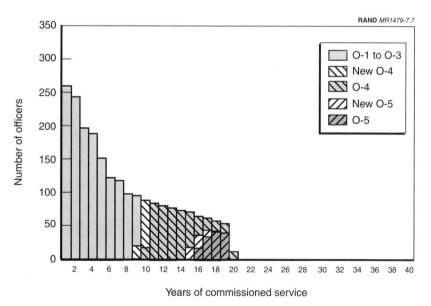

Figure 7.7—Submarine Officers, 2017—In Steady-State

MANAGING THE AVIATION COMMUNITY, 2010 AND 2017

The future aviation community does not present as difficult a management problem as do some of the other communities. The community currently suffers from a shortage of junior officers and an excess of O-4 and O-5 pilots. Because future requirements are posited to be slightly less for junior officers and very slightly higher for O-5 pilots, this problem is somewhat ameliorated. Figure 7.8 shows the steady-state career progression for the aviation community in 2010. It is based on continuation rates very similar to those of today. Pilots are promoted slightly earlier (e.g., to grade O-4 beginning at 10 years of service), and most of those who choose to stay in the service are promoted. Over 80 percent of O-4s are promoted to O-5, beginning at 16 years of service, and a very small number (about a dozen) of selected O-5s remain in service until 30 or 31 years of service. Promotion to O-6 begins at 20 years of service, and approximately 38 percent of eligible O-5s are promoted.

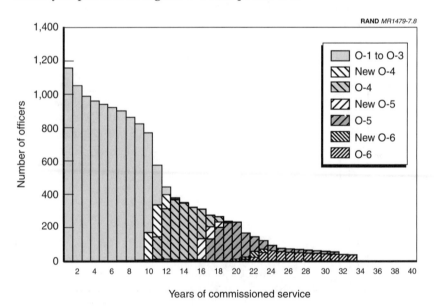

Figure 7.8—Aviation Officers, 2010—In Steady-State

The steady-state representation of the aviation community in 2017 (Figure 7.9) resembles that of 2010 very closely, with only slightly fewer accessions—and the incorporation of the NWI community (Figure 7.5) presenting the only real differences.

MANAGING THE INTELLIGENCE COMMUNITY, 2010 AND 2017

The relatively small intelligence community is currently experiencing a shortage of officers at grades O-4 and above. The requirements posited for 2010 increase current requirements, so the management challenge for this community is how to fill such an increase. Figure 7.10 indicates accessions of approximately 73 officers each year who enter directly into the intelligence community, as well as lateral entries from other naval officer communities. To satisfy the requirements for more senior officers, the career system shown below spreads promotion to O-4 over a period of several years,

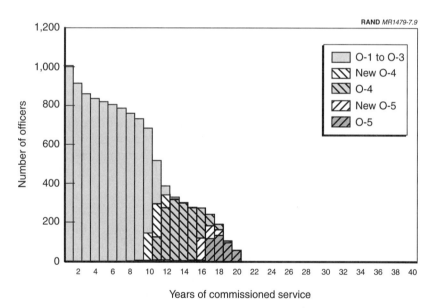

Figure 7.9—Aviation Officers, 2017—In Steady-State

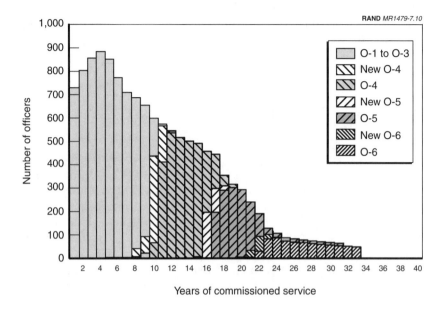

Figure 7.10—Intelligence Officers, 2010—In Steady-State

beginning as early as eight years of service, and almost every officer considered for promotion is promoted. Approximately 65 percent of officers considered are promoted to O-5, beginning in the 16th year of service. A very small number of O-5s (as few as one or two from each year group) continue on active duty as long as 31 years of service. Nonetheless, almost two-thirds of officers considered for promotion to O-6 are promoted to captain, and they tend to remain in the service until about 33 years of service.

By 2017, the intelligence community will see slight decreases, and the management of the system will not change much to meet the posited requirements. Figure 7.11 shows an intelligence community with slightly fewer accessions than in 2010. As before, all officers who remain in the system will be promoted to O-4, and there will also be high promotion to the grades of O-5 (almost 70 percent) and to O-6 (more than half). As before, the intelligence community will continue to see longer careers for a very small number of senior officers.

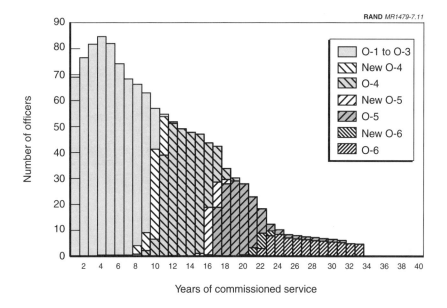

Figure 7.11—Intelligence Officers, 2017—In Steady-State

MANAGING THE SUPPLY COMMUNITY, 2010 AND 2017

The supply community has seen a long-term drop in accessions, with a slight correction in the late 1990s. Extrapolating the current accession rates, given current continuation rates, suggests that there will be a severe shortage of supply officers in grades O-4 to O-6 once the last of the large cohort groups moves through the system. Because the supply community is posited to decrease by only 2 percent between 2001 and 2010, the likely shortage needs to be resolved with either improved continuation rates or increased accessions. Figure 7.12 indicates one steady-state solution for this community in 2010. Accession is only about 210 officers each year, but the continuation rates are increased slightly from years of service 5–12. This behavioral change may require adjusted compensation packages in order to occur. Promotion to O-4 comes a year early for most, and is practically guaranteed for those who do not leave. Promotion rates to

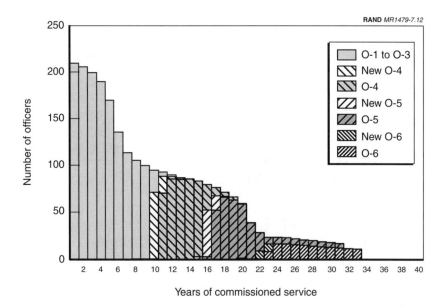

Figure 7.12—Supply Officers, 2010—In Steady-State

O-5 are also high (over 80 percent), and approximately a third of officers considered are promoted to O-6. A few O-5s remain in the service as long as 31 years. The alternative to this solution—increasing
accession—would require about 625 accessions annually to satisfy
the eventual O-4 to O-6 requirements. Such a solution would result
in a 300 percent overage of junior officers.

By 2017, the supply community will have decreased another 4 percent from 2010. These changes have little effect, and the system in
Figure 7.13 is similar to that shown previously. More O-5s are
encouraged to stay for longer careers—to 31 years of commissioned
service—and one result is that the promotion rate to O-5 decreases
to approximately 72 percent. However, the smaller number of O-5s
competing for promotion to O-6 raises those promotion rates to
almost 40 percent.

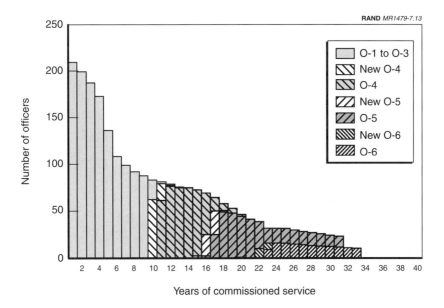

RAND MR1479-7.13

Legend:
- O-1 to O-3
- New O-4
- O-4
- New O-5
- O-5
- New O-6
- O-6

Figure 7.13—Supply Officers, 2017—In Steady-State

COMPARISON OF MANPOWER POLICY CHANGES

Table 7.1 summarizes the policies employed in the steady-state career systems discussed above as compared with current practice. In general, the accessions for each community decrease. This is largely attributed to a management strategy that addresses shortages of midcareer officers in ways other than those used by the current system: increasing accessions and thus suffering the overages of junior officers. Promotion timing varies by community, but the broader zones permit some fast-tracking while keeping officers competitive and considered for longer periods of time. The effects of these different promotion systems for the communities are apparent when examining the promotion opportunities. While actual promotion rates currently vary (as shown in the table entries for "current," which were calculated from actual officer records), future promotion rates could vary considerably more among the communities. For example, the biggest difference is the current rate of promotion to

Table 7.1

Summary of Policies and Outcomes in Future and Current Career Systems, by Community

Policy	Surface Warfare	Submarine	Aviation	Supply	Intelligence
Accessions					
Current	~1,115	~367	~1,194	~219	~82[a]
2010	~685	~300	~1,150	~210	~75
2017	~590	~260	~1,000	~210	~69
Promotion Timing					
Current	YOS 10–12	YOS 10–12	YOS 10–12	YOS 11–12	YOS 10–11
	YOS 16–17	YOS 16–17	YOS 16–17	YOS 16–17	YOS 16–17
	YOS 22–23	YOS 22–23	YOS 22–23	YOS 22–23	YOS 22–23
2010	YOS 7–11	YOS 9–10	YOS 9–12	YOS 10–13	YOS 8–12
	YOS 15–17	YOS 15–17	YOS 16–18	YOS 15–18	YOS 16–18
	YOS 20–27	YOS 21–24	YOS 20–23	YOS 22–23	YOS 20–23
2017	YOS 7–11	YOS 9–10	YOS 10–12	YOS 10–13	YOS 8–12
	YOS 15–17	YOS 15–17	YOS 16–18	YOS 15–18	YOS 15–18
	YOS 20–23[c]	YOS 20–23[c]	YOS 20–23[c]	YOS 22–23	YOS 20–23
Promotion Opportunity					
Current[b]	61% (O-4)	76% (O-4)	65% (O-4)	70% (O-4)	69% (O-4)
	69% (O-5)	65% (O-5)	60% (O-5)	72% (O-5)	67% (O-5)
	55% (O-6)	57% (O-6)	53% (O-6)	53% (O-6)	69% (O-6)
2010	72% (O-4)	94% (O-4)	55% (O-4)	94% (O-4)	92% (O-4)
	86% (O-5)	64% (O-5)	81% (O-5)	83% (O-5)	65% (O-5)
	72% (O-6)	50% (O-6)	38% (O-6)	30% (O-6)	39% (O-6)

Table 7.1—continued

Policy	Surface Warfare	Submarine	Aviation	Supply	Intelligence
2017	69% (O-4)	92% (O-4)	53% (O-4)	95% (O-4)	91% (O-4)
	88% (O-5)	67% (O-5)	83% (O-5)	72% (O-5)	65% (O-5)
	79% (O-6)[c]	79% (O-6)[c]	79% (O-6)[c]	38% (O-6)	39% (O-6)
Allowed Service					
Current	O-4 20 YOS	O-4 20 YOS	O-4 20 YOS	O-4 20 YOS	O-4 20 YOS
	O-5 28 YOS	O-5 28 YOS	O-5 28 YOS	O-5 28 YOS	O-5 28 YOS
	O-6 30 YOS	O-6 30 YOS	O-6 30 YOS	O-6 30 YOS	O-6 30 YOS
2010	O-4 20 YOS	O-4 20 YOS	O-4 20 YOS	O-4 20 YOS	O-4 20 YOS
	O-5 31 YOS	O-5 31 YOS	O-5 31 YOS	O-5 31 YOS	O-5 31 YOS
	O-6 33 YOS	O-6 35 YOS	O-6 33 YOS	O-6 33 YOS	O-6 33 YOS
2017	O-4 20 YOS	O-4 20 YOS	O-4 20 YOS	O-4 20 YOS	O-4 20 YOS
	O-5 to NWI	O-5 to NWI	O-5 to NWI	O-5 31 YOS	O-5 31 YOS
	by 21 YOS[d]	by 19 YOS[d]	by 20 YOS[d]	O-6 33 YOS	O-6 33 YOS
Average Experience					
Current	8.40	9.74	9.30	10.80	9.94
2010	9.15	10.16	9.10	10.13	10.43
2017	6.65	7.46	8.09	10.65	10.42

[a] In YOS 1. More officers laterally transfer to intelligence in ensuing YOS.
[b] Calculated from historical data using formula consistent with model estimates.
[c] Promotion occurs after lateral transfer to NWI. Surface warfare, submarine, and aviation rates are not calculated separately.
[d] NWI allowed service is shown in Figure 7.5.

O-6. Aviation and supply officers have been promoted at a rate of approximately 53 percent, while intelligence officers enjoy a 69 percent promotion to O-6. Nonetheless, this is only a 16-point difference. In future officer management systems, if the communities are managed to requirements, promotion rates could vary by approximately 40 percentage points from one community to another. In some instances, this reflects relatively low promotion rates in a community. In other instances, the low end approximates the current system, while the high end results from a particular community promoting almost everyone. Another change is reflected in the number of years an officer could serve within a grade, which would be extended several years for selected O-5s and O-6s in most communities.

This table summarizes the results of the model runs, which simulated the steady-state management of officers to meet posited requirements by community. However, these results are dynamic in that a change to any policy depicted here will change other recommended policies. If, for example, the promotion rates were made more similar across communities, the promotion timing and allowed service would likely also change. If continuation rates changed dramatically, then that behavior would affect policy choices.

It is not so much the particular policies that are of interest themselves, but that these differing policies point to broad considerations of a changed management system. We have asserted elsewhere that such a system needs to be strategic, systemic, and more flexible than uniform. Given the different grade structures of the various communities and the different continuation behavior of different kinds of officers, if the Navy chooses to reduce manpower gaps by managing to requirements, then communities will need to be managed separately. The extent to which policies differ (and are perceived to differ) among communities will potentially affect behavior until expectations alter to match the system. Reconsideration of these policy choices, given changes in behavior, will need to include an examination of the policies as interactive sets of decisions.

SUMMARY

Previous RAND research has prescribed the rationale and methods for officer management. Management of the officer corps needs to be both strategic and systemic. Moreover, decisions need to be made about the amount of uniformity across occupations as well as the amount of flexibility in design.

The issue of strategy is largely that of being tied to future mission needs and being an active instrument of the Navy's overall strategy for the future. Officer management should play a more positive role in planning rather than the largely constraining one that it seems to play currently. In other words, to the extent possible, the Navy should be trying to shape—size and composition—the future officer corps toward mission need and desired outcomes instead of largely reacting to past changes to the internal and external environment.

The issue of being systemic is that the management structure must work as a system. Accession is not a separately planned function from retention and retirement. The entire process of entering officers and then training, educating, promoting, assigning, developing, and separating them must be viewed as an interlinked system. There must be internal consistency among the functional parts of the system, and the system must accommodate and balance the needs of multiple stakeholders—the Navy overall, units and organizations that use officers to accomplish missions and workload, and individual officers. This is not to say that at various times certain functions may receive more or less attention than other functions. But there must be recognition that changes in one functional area can affect the entire system.

The issue of uniformity has to do with whether centralized approaches to officer management that best suit dominant Navy occupations hinder the Navy's ability to manage other occupations. Should different occupational groups be managed differently? To prosper in an increasingly complex internal and external environment, the Navy might need to become less uniform and more specialized in approach.

Last, an agency must imbue any personnel management structure with sufficient flexibility to respond to the types of changes that have occurred and will occur. Trends are at work and cycles are inevitable

as economic conditions and national priorities change. Instilling
flexibility might involve fewer central policy prescriptions and fewer
central controls. The policy rules of the road might need to be broad-
ened to allow more freedom of movement for managing officers and
for individuals within the system to meet their own needs. However,
there may be negative, as well as positive, consequences associated
with deregulating and decentralizing a personnel system, for example, diminished Navy identity, increased rivalries among organizations and occupational groups, less ability to work together, and less
understanding of one another's mission or the "common" interest.
These consequences must be either avoided or mitigated or accepted
culturally.

Chapter Eight

CONCLUSIONS AND RECOMMENDATIONS

CONCLUSIONS

Analysis of historic manning data indicates that the organization of work and the composition of the military force changes with mission, organization, and technology. Some analyses attempt to capture these changes and then characterize the Navy with tooth-to-tail comparisons. However, such distinctions are analytically clouded, confused by multiple definitions, and loaded with pejorative interpretations.

There are multiple reasons why communities have manning shortages or excesses at various grades. Authorizations can change instantaneously; however, inventory cannot. The system can react most quickly to large-scale changes at the junior grades. Additionally, changing accession group sizes appears to be a common approach to resolving manning shortages or excesses elsewhere in the system, even if the result is an excess of junior officers. Thus, these grades are likely to show the greatest fluctuation in inventory. However, large fluctuations result in varying sizes of cohort groups moving through the closed system. While external constraints or controls can affect the level of authorizations within communities, these cohorts will present management hurdles within the current cohort (year group)–based system.

Finally, the grade structures of some communities are inherently easier to manage. The grade structures of some communities suggest perpetual overages (such as with senior doctors), while other communities (such as the submarine community) are shaped by almost unattainable grade structures. The latter suggests the need to reevaluate the proportionate grade structure for such communities. Absent the changes that permit management of Navy manning by community and provide relief from DOPMA constraints, manning gaps are inevitable in most communities under the present system.

There are both hard (dollar) costs and soft (nondollar) costs associated with manning overages and shortages, and these costs differ by each community, given different manning gaps. Hard costs are more easily identified, and include dollar costs or savings associated with compensation, and accession and training costs. Soft costs are more difficult to identify and quantify. Examples of soft costs include lower performance because of lack of training, motivation, or other deficiencies; readiness problems as a result of uncompleted work or low retention; and low workforce task cohesion resulting from instability among a crew. In the short term, these soft costs are measured by factors other than dollars, if measured at all.

The Navy has not traditionally considered individual costs by community when programming manpower, and has instead used a single programming cost for all officers. This process obscures the actual cost of manning and the fact that different communities have different development and compensation costs. Recognizing these differences permits a more accurate evaluation of the effects of dollar costs from manpower gaps and implies inefficiencies in the system.

With the exception of the intelligence community and the Medical Corps, most communities cycle in a narrow band around the $0 gridline for costs and savings because of manpower gaps. Sometimes they cost and at other times they save, but in general they are within a likely management tolerance, which is not inconsistent with the friction of managing inventory in a closed system. The intelligence community, which has seen relatively little change in its chronic undermanning, consistently has "savings"—less dollar costs than planned. However, the Medical Corps has decreased its long-standing undermanning and currently costs slightly more than planned. Excluding the aviation community, the communities analyzed have generally become, when averaged together, more costly to the Navy each year since 1988—in essence, the savings disappear over time—as undermanning, especially in the highest-cost medical community, has been reduced.

While the sum of manning costs for most communities is close to planned costs, this is because manning excesses and shortages within the communities tend to cancel one another out for costing purposes. Analysis of the costs and savings within each community provides considerable insights. For example, the Navy appears either to be using more senior officers to fly planes in lieu of more junior officers or to be using these senior officers as excess staff or to staff disproportionately 1000/1050 billets. Either way, the savings from not having junior officers are reduced by having too many senior officers. Moreover, such long-standing "savings" begin to prompt the question whether these missing officers are needed at all, or if they existed, could they be afforded? Also, the entire system, year by year, nets its costs and savings to an overall savings, which indicates that having fewer pilots than planned each year helps to fund the inefficiencies elsewhere in the system, particularly for SWOs.

Analysis of the actual costs of gaps also suggests that the grade structure and experience patterns of some communities should be rethought. For example, shortages in junior (O-1 and O-2) aviation officers have consistently resulted in lower-than-planned manning costs for the aviation community. Since 1994, the savings associated with paygrades O-1 to O-2 have decreased while those of O-3 have increased. The cost of producing O-1s and O-2s is very high, so "savings" dissipate quickly as O-1 and O-2 undermanning decreases. Thus, finding a way to keep more expensively trained officers longer (pilots currently have a longer service commitment than other officers) can be useful if it means avoiding training costs. The marginal grade-to-grade costs are small compared with the initial cost of training an officer.

The pattern by grade in the intelligence community is relatively consistent over time, resulting in consistent dollar savings for this community (Figure 5.8). Are all the authorizations truly needed if they are so consistently undermanned? Perversely, removing such authorizations would increase dollar costs in the short term but ameliorate the softer costs in the longer term.

There are inherent difficulties in any effort to forecast future requirements or billets authorized. Our posited future scenarios are used in this report to provide a target set of authorizations to test various manpower policies. In general, the modeling concluded that the communities must be managed separately to meet requirements better. Management policies that vary by community include promotion timing, the number promoted to each grade, and allowed career length.

While this report provides a set of management policies for each community that permits attainment of the posited requirements, each set is changeable and dynamic. We provide only one set of policy changes that work together to create a coherent career structure. The various policies can be changed beyond what this report suggests. Even longer careers are possible, given that the impact on promotion opportunities and timing is acceptable. Likewise, promotion opportunities can almost always be increased, given that the impact on promotion timing is palatable. The interactive and dynamic nature of these policies underscores the need for a flexible, responsive system that manages communities individually to their requirements.

RECOMMENDATIONS

We recommend that the Navy consider the following:

- Pursue legislative relief from DOPMA or change in DoD policy that will permit the Navy to manage communities by requirements. Such management would minimize manpower gaps and decrease both hard costs associated with overmanning as well as soft costs associated with either positive or negative gaps.

- Manage communities flexibly and individually, employing management tools such as longer careers (for small numbers of senior personnel as well as for O-3 and O-4 officers) and broader promotion zones as needed in each community to match inventory to requirements. Managing communities optimally would also require legislative relief from DOPMA.

- Acknowledge that the existing grade structure for some communities, such as submarine and intelligence officer communities, is inherently insupportable. Either revisit the proportionate structure of these communities or pursue management tools (e.g., longer times in grade, greater use of LDOs) that will enable the Navy to satisfy these requirements.

- Restructure the management of LDOs. LDOs should be managed within the officer community that they are associated with and should be considered a manpower tool to meet the requirements of that community rather than as a separate community in and of themselves. Their retention behavior is consistent with, and can resolve potential gaps in, the manpower requirements of most communities that need greater retention from 6 to 12 years after commissioning.

- Consider the costs of manpower, by community and grade, in the manpower planning process and when determining and filling requirements. For example, unless there are valid needs, requirements for aviators and submariners apart from ship and aviation manning documents should be minimized. Also, assigning aviators and submariners to 1000/1050 billets should be a last choice. The availability of such officers to staff such billets indicates an oversupply of this high-priced resource. In a system where officers are managed to requirements, one less requirement for an aviator will result in one less aviator in the system. This encourages the use of other, less-expensive officers to staff billets that do not specifically need high-priced expertise.

- Similarly, recognize that training fewer officers initially but keeping more of those trained through incentives may be desirable. In essence, the cost of a higher-graded authorization offsets the cost of training a new O-1. Suggestions of this type need to be evaluated in more detail.

- Consider more integrative communities for future manpower needs to reflect and accommodate changes in the force structure as well as recommendations by the Quadrennial Defense Review and likely technological advances, such as network-centric warfare.

NAVY OFFICER PROGRAMMED AUTHORIZATION PREDICTIONS BY COMMUNITY

These figures demonstrate the inherent weaknesses of manpower forecasting by displaying the Officer Programmed Authorization (OPA) predictions in five-year increments, compared with the actual Billets Authorized (BA) over the period forecasted. These figures are not meant to imply that the forecasts displayed remained static, as OPA revisions occur three times annually. These figures are intended only to demonstrate the difficulty in forecasting the future of manpower communities.

As an example, Figure A.1 indicates the OPA five-year forecasts made in fiscal years 1988, 1991, 1995, and 2000. The stars represent the year the estimates were made; the bars of the same shade as the stars indicate later years of that same forecast. A change in shading indicates a new OPA examined.

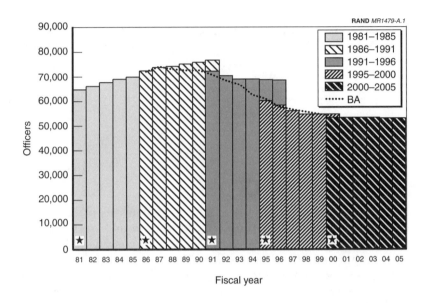

Figure A.1—Total Navy OPA Predictions Compared with Actual BA

Figures A.2–A.6 indicate the OPA predictions and actual BA for selected communities. The communities differ in whether they overestimate or underestimate BA, and in which periods they were more or less accurate. For example, the surface warfare community consistently overestimated manpower, whereas the submarine community overestimated manpower only in their FY 1991 OPA. Further, of the communities considered, only the submarine community and the aviation community underestimated manpower in their FY 1995 OPA. Interestingly, although the previous chapter indicated that the supply community experienced the least dramatic gaps throughout their grades, their forecasting estimations were less accurate than most other communities considered (second only to the surface warfare community).

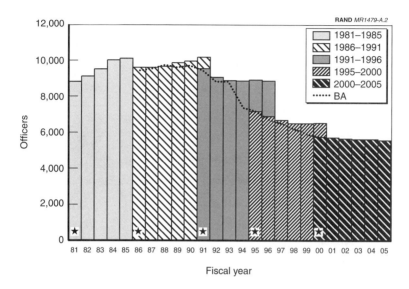

**Figure A.2—Surface Warfare Community OPA Predictions Compared
with Actual BA**

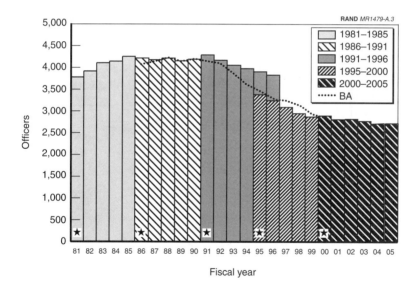

**Figure A.3—Submarine Community OPA Predictions Compared
with Actual BA**

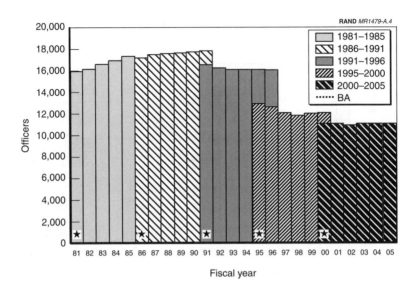

Figure A.4—Aviation Community OPA Predictions Compared
with Actual BA

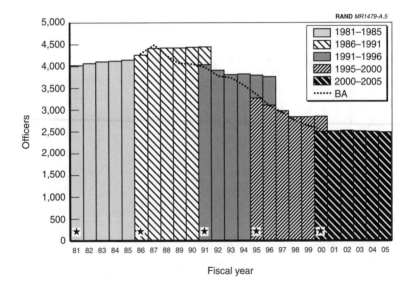

Figure A.5—Supply Community OPA Predictions Compared
with Actual BA

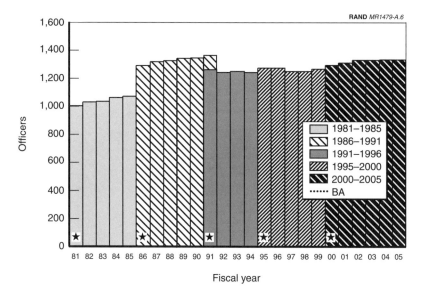

**Figure A.6—Intelligence Community OPA Predictions Compared
with Actual BA**

NAVY PROGRAM OF RECORD,
FISCAL YEARS 2000–2010

Table B.1

Navy Program of Record, Fiscal Years 2000–2010

	Fiscal Year										
	2000	2001	2002	2003	2004	2005	2006	2007	2008	2009	2010
Amphibs											
LHD-1	6	7	7	7	7	7	7	7	7	7	7
LH(X)	0	0	0	0	0	0	0	0	0	0	0
LHA	5	5	5	5	5	5	5	5	5	5	5
LPH2	0	0	0	0	0	0	0	0	0	0	0
LSD36	3	3	3	3	3	2	1	1	0	0	0
LSD41/49	12	12	12	12	12	12	12	12	12	12	12
LSD(X)	0	0	0	0	0	0	0	0	0	0	0
LPD4	11	11	11	10	9	7	5	3	1	0	0
LPD17	0	0	0	2	3	5	7	10	12	12	12
LST 1179	2	2	2	2	2	2	1	0	0	0	0
Total	39	40	40	41	41	40	38	38	37	36	36
Surface Combat											
CGN-36	0	0	0	0	0	0	0	0	0	0	0
CGN-38	0	0	0	0	0	0	0	0	0	0	0
CG-47	27	27	27	27	27	27	27	27	27	27	27
CG-21	0	0	0	0	0	0	0	0	0	0	0
DD-963	24	21	19	19	16	13	10	7	3	3	0

Table B.1—continued

	Fiscal Year										
	2000	2001	2002	2003	2004	2005	2006	2007	2008	2009	2010
DDG-993	0	0	0	0	0	0	0	0	0	0	0
DDG-51	30	33	37	40	43	46	49	52	56	57	57
DD21	0	0	0	0	0	0	0	0	1	4	7
FFG-7	35	35	33	30	30	30	30	30	29	25	25
Total	116	116	116	116	116	116	116	116	116	116	116
Carrier											
CV59/60/62	0	0	0	0	0	0	0	0	0	0	0
CV63/67	3	3	3	2	2	2	2	2	1	1	1
CVN65	1	1	1	1	1	1	1	1	1	1	1
CVN68-77	8	8	8	9	9	9	9	9	10	10	10
CVX	0	0	0	0	0	0	0	0	0	0	0
Total	12	12	12	12	12	12	12	12	12	12	12
CLF											
T/AE26	7	7	7	7	7	7	7	6	4	2	0
AO177	0	0	0	0	0	0	0	0	0	0	0
TAO187	13	13	13	13	13	13	13	13	13	13	13
TA0(X)	0	0	0	0	0	0	0	0	0	0	0
AOE6	4	4	4	4	4	4	4	4	4	4	4
AOE1	4	4	4	4	4	4	4	4	2	1	0

Table B.1—continued

	Fiscal Year										
	2000	2001	2002	2003	2004	2005	2006	2007	2008	2009	2010
T/ADCX	0	0	0	0	0	2	3	6	9	11	12
T/AFS1	3	3	3	3	3	1	0	0	0	0	0
TAFS8	3	3	3	3	3	3	3	1	0	0	0
Total	34	34	34	34	34	34	34	34	32	31	29
Support											
AS33/36	0	0	0	0	0	0	0	0	0	0	0
AS39	2	2	2	2	2	2	2	2	2	2	2
AS(X)	0	0	0	0	0	0	0	0	0	0	0
ARS50	4	4	4	4	4	4	4	4	4	4	4
TATF166	7	7	7	7	7	7	7	7	7	7	7
TATF(X)	0	0	0	0	0	0	0	0	0	0	0
TAGOS1-18	3	3	3	3	3	3	3	3	3	3	3
TAGOS19	4	4	4	4	4	4	4	4	4	4	4
TAGOS23	1	1	1	1	1	1	1	1	1	1	1
Total	21	21	21	21	21	21	21	21	21	21	21
Submarine											
SSBN 726 OHIO	18	18	18	16	14	14	14	14	14	14	14
SSBNX	0	0	0	0	0	0	0	0	0	0	0
SSGN	0	0	0	0	0	0	0	0	0	0	0

Table B.1—continued

	Fiscal Year										
	2000	2001	2002	2003	2004	2005	2006	2007	2008	2009	2010
SSN21	2	2	2	3	3	3	3	3	3	3	3
NSSN	0	0	0	0	1	2	2	3	4	4	5
SSN(X)	0	0	0	0	0	0	0	0	0	0	0
SSN688	51	50	47	47	47	46	45	44	43	43	42
SSN671	0	0	0	0	0	0	0	0	0	0	0
SSN637	2	1	1	1	0	0	0	0	0	0	0
SSN640	1	1	0	0	0	0	0	0	0	0	0
Total	74	72	68	67	65	65	64	64	64	64	64
MIW											
MCM1	14	14	14	14	14	14	14	14	14	14	14
MCM(X)	0	0	0	0	0	0	0	0	0	0	0
MHC50	1	1	1	1	1	1	1	1	1	1	1
MHC(X)	0	0	0	0	0	0	0	0	0	0	0
Total	15	15	15	15	15	15	15	15	15	15	15
Command Ships											
MCS	1	1	1	1	1	1	1	1	1	1	1
AGF11	1	1	1	1	1	1	1	1	1	0	0
AGF3	1	1	1	1	1	1	1	1	1	0	0
LCC	2	2	2	2	2	2	2	2	2	2	1

Table B.1—continued

	Fiscal Year										
	2000	2001	2002	2003	2004	2005	2006	2007	2008	2009	2010
LCC(X)	0	0	0	0	0	0	0	0	0	2	3
Total	5	5	5	5	5	5	5	5	5	5	5
Overall Total	316	315	311	311	309	308	305	305	302	300	298

BIBLIOGRAPHY

99th Congress, First Session, *Defense Organization: The Need for Change*, Senate Print 99-86, Committee on Armed Services, United States Senate, October 16, 1985.

_____, Second Session, *Department of Defense Reorganization Act of 1986*, P.L. 99-433, in *United States Code Congressional and Administrative News*, Volume 1, St. Paul, Minn.: West Publishing Co., 1986.

_____, Second Session, *Legislative History: Department of Defense Reorganization Act of 1986*, in *United States Code Congressional and Administrative News*, Volume 4, St. Paul, Minn.: West Publishing Co., 1986.

_____, Second Session, *Reorganization of the Department of Defense: Hearings Before the Investigations Subcommittee of the Committee on Armed Services*, HASC No. 99-53, United States House of Representatives, 1987.

100th Congress, First Session, *Department of Defense Authorization Act for Fiscal Year 1988*, P.L. 100-180, in *United States Code Congressional and Administrative News*, Volume 1, St. Paul, Minn.: West Publishing Co., 1987.

_____, Second Session, *National Defense Authorization Act for Fiscal Year 1989: Report of the Committee on Armed Services*, United States House of Representatives, Report 100-563, April 4, 1988.

_____, Second Session, *Department of Defense Authorization Act for Fiscal Year 1989*, P.L. 100-456, in *United States Code Congressional and Administrative News*, Volume 1, St. Paul, Minn.: West Publishing Co., 1988.

101st Congress, First Session, *Department of Defense Authorization Act for Fiscal Year 1990*, P.L. 101-189, in *United States Code Congressional and Administrative News*, Volume 1, St. Paul, Minn.: West Publishing Co., 1989.

102nd Congress, Second Session, *Department of Defense Authorization Act for Fiscal Year 1990*, P.L. 102-484, in *United States Code Congressional and Administrative News*, Volume 2, St. Paul, Minn.: West Publishing Co., 1992.

103rd Congress, First Session, *National Defense Authorization Act for Fiscal Year 1994: Report to the Committee on Armed Services*, United States Senate, Report 103-112, July 27, 1993.

_____, First Session, *National Defense Authorization Act for Fiscal Year 1994: Conference Report to Accompany H.R. 2401*, United States House of Representatives, Report 103-357, November 10, 1993.

104th Congress, Second Session, *National Defense Authorization Act for Fiscal Year 1997*, United States Senate, Report 104-267, May 13, 1996.

Anderberg, Michael R., *Cluster Analysis for Applications*, New York: Academic Press, 1973.

Assistant Secretary of Defense (Manpower, Reserve Affairs, and Logistics), *Assignment of Joint Tours of Duty*, Department of Defense Directive 1320.5, July 26, 1978.

Assistant Secretary of Defense (Force Management and Policy), *Joint Duty Positions Pertaining to Title IV of the DoD Reorganization Act*, Memorandum for the Under Secretaries of Defense, Washington, D.C., December 4, 1986.

_____, *Report on the Study of Joint Officer Management Initiatives*, Washington, D.C., April 1990.

_____, *Restructured Joint Officer Program,* Memorandum for the Assistant Secretary of the Army (Manpower and Reserve Affairs), Washington, D.C., November 18, 1991.

Blanco, Thomas, "Report of Workshop: Requirements," Center for Naval Analyses, 1982.

Bowes, Marianne, and Janet Thomason, *The Use of Requirements Data in Models of the Enlisted Force,* CRM 89- 57, Center for Naval Analyses, September 1989.

Brown, David, "Skeleton Crew: Destroyers with 95 Crew Members? Tech Teams Tell How That Might Happen," *Navy Times,* June 4, 2001, p. 12. Available at http://www.ncmanational.org/sit_01.html (last accessed August 7, 2002).

Carl, Brauna, *CNO Announces Plans to Align the Fleet,* Navy Office of Information, August 22, 2001. Available at http://www.navy.mil/.

Chairman of the Joint Chiefs of Staff, *Implementation of Title IV: DoD Reorganization Act,* Memorandum, CM-683-87, April 14, 1987.

_____, *Report on the Roles, Missions, and Functions of the Armed Forces of the United States,* CM-1584-93, February 1993.

_____, *Military Education Policy Document,* CM-1618-93, March 23, 1993.

_____, *Review of Promotion Selection Board Results by the Chairman of the Joint Chiefs of Staff,* Instruction, CJCSI 1330.02, January 7, 1994.

_____, *Joint Manpower Program Procedures,* CJCSM 1600.01, April 30, 1998.

_____, *Officer Professional Military Education Policy,* Instruction, CJCSI 1800.01A, December 1, 2000.

_____, *Policy and Procedures to Assign Individuals to Meet Combatant Command Mission-Related Temporary Duty Requirements,* Instruction, CJCSI 1301.01B, May 1, 2001.

_____, *Assignment of Officers (0-6 and Below) to the Joint Staff,* Instruction, CJCSI 1330.01B, June 4, 2001.

Chief of Naval Operations, *Top Five Priorities* ("Manpower" section) United States Navy. Available at http://www.chinfo.navy.mil/ navpalib/cno/cno-top5manpwr.html (last accessed August 7, 2002).

Chisholm, Donald, *Waiting for Dead Men's Shoes: Origins and Development of the U.S. Navy's Officer Personnel System, 1793– 1941,* Stanford, Calif.: Stanford University Press, 2001.

Clark, Vern, "Remarks to the Surface Navy Association National Symposium," Arlington, Va., January 10, 2001. Available at http://www.navy.mil/.

_____, "Current Strategy Forum," Newport, R.I., June 12, 2001. Available at http://www.navy.mil/.

Coats, Lieutenant Colonel Julius E., *Joint Duty Prerequisite for Promotion to O-7 (Brigadier General)*, Carlisle Barracks, Pa.: U.S. Army War College, March 13, 1989.

Colvard, James E., Carolyn Ban, Madelyn P. Jennings, James L. Perry, and Curtis J. Smith (panel members), *Civilian Workforce 2020: Strategies for Modernizing Human Resources Management in the Department of the Navy,* Washington, D.C.: National Academy of Public Administration, August 18, 2001.

Committee on Armed Services, United States House of Representatives, *Report of the Panel on Military Education of the One Hundredth Congress* [The Skelton Report], 101st Congress, First Session, Committee Print No. 4, April 21, 1989.

Congressional Budget Office, *Manpower for a 600-Ship Navy: Costs and Policy Alternatives,* Washington, D.C., August 1983.

Crawley, James W., "S.D. Admirals to Play Role in Navy's Move to Meld Fleets," *San Diego Union-Tribune,* September 4, 2001, p. B3.

Dalton, John H., J. M. Boorda, and Carl E. Mundy Jr., *Forward . . . From the Sea,* Washington, D.C.: Department of the Navy, 1994.

Department of Defense, *Guidance for Manpower Programs,* Directive No. 1100.4, August 20, 1954.

_____, *Military-Civilian Staffing of Management Positions in the Support Activities,* Directive No. 1100.9, September 8, 1971.

_____, *Security Assistance Technical Assistance Field Teams (TAFTs),* Directive No. 5132.10, December 14, 1973.

_____, *Defense Manpower Requirements Report (DMRR),* No. 1110.1, June 28, 1979.

_____, *Programming and Accounting for Active Military Manpower,* Instruction No. 1120.11, April 9, 1981.

_____, *Manpower Requirements Report FY 1986, Volume III: Force Readiness Report,* February 1985.

_____, *Manning of Security Assistance Organizations and the Selection and USDP Training of Security Assistance Personnel,* Directive No. 2055.3, March 11, 1985.

_____, *Military Personnel Assignments,* Directive No. 1315.7, January 9, 1987.

_____, *Defense Officer Requirements Study,* March 1988.

_____, *Defense Acquisition Education, Training, and Career Development Program,* Directive No. 5000.52, October 25, 1991.

_____, *Department of Defense Support Activities (DSAs),* Directive No. 5100.81, December 5, 1991.

_____, *Defense Acquisition Workforce,* Instruction No. 5000.58, January 14, 1992.

_____, *Manpower Requirements Report FY 1993: Officer Flow Annex,* February 1992.

_____, *Manpower Requirements Report, Manpower Flow Annex, FY 1994,* June 1993.

_____, *Manpower Requirements Report FY 1996,* March 1995 (DMRR, 1995).

_____, *Secretary of Defense Fellows Program,* Directive No. 1322.23, September 2, 1995.

_____, *DoD Joint Officer Management Program Procedures*, Instruction No. 1300.20, December 20, 1996.

_____, *Detail of DoD Personnel to Duty Outside the Department of Defense*, Directive No. 1000.17, February 24, 1997.

_____, *Fellowships, Scholarships, and Grants for DoD Personnel*, Directive No. 1322.6, February 24, 1997.

_____, *DoD Joint Officer Management Program*, Directive No. 1300.19, September 9, 1997.

_____, *Director of Administration and Management (DA&M)*, Directive No. 5105.53, November 23, 1998.

_____, *Washington Headquarters Services (WHS)*, Directive No. 5110.4, May 10, 1999.

_____, *Defense Manpower Requirements Report: Fiscal Year 2001*, Prepared by Office of the Under Secretary of Defense for Personnel and Readiness OUSD(PI)(RQ), May 2000.

_____, *Future Years Defense Program (FYDP) Structure Handbook*, DoD 7045.7-H, November 2000.

_____, "DoD News Briefing—Dr. David S.C. Chu, USD (Personnel & Readiness)," News Transcript, August 8, 2001. Available at http://www.defenselink.mil/news/Aug2001/t08082001_t0808chu.html (last accessed August 7, 2002).

_____, *Quadrennial Defense Review Report*, September 30, 2001.

_____, "Navy Announces DD(X) Program," News Release, No. 559-0, November 1, 2001. Available at http://www.defenselink.mil/news/nov2001/b11012001_bt559-01.html (last accessed August 7, 2002).

Department of the Navy, *CNA Report 58, Conference Proceedings: Naval Manpower Research in the 1980's*, Ser 91/3U334713, July 1, 1983.

_____(Commander Naval Surface Force, United States Atlantic Fleet), *Smart Ship Project Assessment Report*, http://www.dt.navy.mil/smartship/assess0997.html, 3980 Ser N6/1687, September 9, 1997.

_____, Fiscal Year (FY) 2001 Budget Estimates, *Justification of Estimates February 2000.*

_____, *Manual of Navy Officer Manpower and Personnel Classifications* NAVPERS 15839I, Volumes I and II, April 2001.

_____(N81 Assessment Division), *Manpower and Personnel: Joint Manpower Requirements Determination, Briefing,* July 24, 2001.

_____(Office of the Chief of Naval Operations), *The U.S. Navy Personnel Exchange Program,* OPNAV Instruction No. 5700.7G, April 29, 1991.

_____(Office of the Chief of Naval Operations), *Projected Operations Environment for DDG-51 (Arleigh Burke) Class Guided Missile Destroyers,* OPNAV Instruction No. 3501.311A, Draft, June 30, 1997.

_____(Office of the Chief of Naval Operations), *Manpower Requirements and Authorizations Procedures,* OPNAVINST 1000.16J N121, January 6, 1998.

_____(Office of the Chief of Naval Operations), *Enlisted Military Personnel Navy (MPN) Programmed Authorizations for Fiscal Years 1999–2004,* Ser N122E2C/9U00175, October 21, 1999.

_____(Office of the Chief of Naval Operations), *Individual Augmentation (IA) Policy and Procedures,* Department of Defense Directives, OPNAVINST 1001.24 N512H, July 5, 2000.

_____(Office of the Chief of Naval Operations), *Officer Military Personnel Navy (MPN) Programmed Authorizations for Fiscal Year 2000–2005,* 1000 Ser 122E1C/0U0150, October 10, 2000.

_____(Office of the Chief of Naval Operations), *Manual of Navy Officer Manpower and Personnel Classifications Volume II,* NAVPERS 158391, April 2001.

_____, *Officer Programmed Authorizations, Fiscal Years 1981–1985,* CNO ltr Ser 122E2/689221, November 20, 1980.

_____, *Officer Programmed Authorizations, Fiscal Years 1986–1991,* CNO ltr Ser 122E2/371134, December 19, 1985.

_____, *Officer Programmed Authorizations, Fiscal Years 1991–1996*, CNO ltr Ser 122E2/0U573578, November 20, 1990.

_____, *Officer Programmed Authorizations, Fiscal Years 1995–2000*, CNO ltr Ser 122E1/5U82734, September 29, 1995.

_____, *Officer Programmed Authorizations, Fiscal Years 2000–2005*, CNO ltr Ser 122E1C/0U0150, October 10, 2000.

_____, *Officer Transfer Manual*, NAVPER 15559B, undated.

_____, *Total Force Manpower Management System (TFMMS) Coding Directory*, NAVPERS 16000A, January 2001.

Deputy Secretary of Defense, *Title IV, DoD Reorganization Act of 1986*, Memorandum for the Secretaries of the Military Departments, Washington, D.C., May 21, 1987.

_____, *Career Guidelines and Oversight Procedures for Joint Specialty Officers and Other Officers Serving in Joint Duty Assignments*, Memorandum for Secretaries of the Military Departments, Washington, D.C., July 22, 1987.

_____, *Scientific and Technical Qualifications List*, Memorandum for the Secretaries of the Military Departments, Washington, D.C., November 20, 1987.

_____, *Additional Guidelines for the Implementation of Title IV, DoD Reorganization Act of 1986*, Memorandum for Secretaries of the Military Departments, Washington, D.C., February 4, 1988.

_____, *Additional Guidelines for Administration of Joint Duty Assignment (JDA) Programs*, Memorandum for the Secretaries of the Military Departments, Washington, D.C., August 22, 1988.

_____, *Revised Definitions for Dual-Hat and Cross-Department Joint Duty Assignments*, Memorandum for Secretaries of the Military Departments, Washington, D.C., February 27, 1989.

_____, *Additional Guidelines for the Implementation and Administration of the Joint Officer Management Programs*, Memorandum for the Secretaries of the Military Departments, Washington, D.C., June 19, 1989.

Eisman, Dale, "Norfolk Admiral Gets More to Do with New Role," *Virginian-Pilot*, August 14, 2001.

Fages, Malcolm, "The Submarine Force: A Century of Excellence, and the Challenge of the Future," *Undersea Warfare*, Vol. 2, No. 4, Summer 2000. Available at http://www.chinfo.navy.mil/navpalib/cno/n87/usw/issue_8/challenge_of_future.html (last accessed August 7, 2002).

Fuller, Craig S., *The Navy and Jointness: No Longer Reluctant Partners?* Thesis, Monterey, Calif.: Naval Postgraduate School, December 1991.

General Accounting Office, *Military Personnel: Options to Implement Officer Reductions*, GAO/NSIAD-87-162, August 1987.

_____, *Military Officers: Assessment of the 1988 Defense Officer Requirements Study*, GAO/NSIAD-88-146, April 1988.

_____, *Military Personnel: Designation of Joint Duty Assignments*, Report to Congressional Requesters, B-232940, February 1990.

_____, *Defense Personnel: Status of Implementing Joint Assignments for Military Leaders*, GAO/NSIAD-91-50BR, January 1991.

_____, *Force Structure: Streamlining Plans Could Enable Navy to Reduce Personnel Below Fiscal Year 1999 Goal*, GAO/NSAID-97-90, April 1997.

_____, *Force Structure: Projected Requirements for Some Army Forces Not Well Established*, GAO-01-485, May 2001.

Goldwater, Barry M., with Jack Casserly, *Goldwater*, New York: Doubleday, 1988 (especially Chapter 11, "Duty-Honor-Country," pp. 334–361).

Goodman, Glenn W., Jr., "Offshore Warriors: Navy's Surface Combatants Set for More Significant Role in Future Joint-Service Operations Overseas," *Armed Forces Journal International*, April 1999, pp. 42–44.

Hagerott, Mark, "It's Time to Think as One Navy," *Proceedings*, Vol. 127, No. 8, August 2001, pp. 58–61.

Hamilton, Robert A., "Advocating a More Nimble Navy," *New London [Conn.] Day*, August 19, 2001.

Harrell, Margaret C., John F. Schank, Harry J. Thie, Clifford M. Graf II, and Paul Steinberg, *How Many Can Be Joint? Supporting Joint Duty Assignments*, Santa Monica, Calif.: RAND, MR-593-JS, 1996.

Harrell, Margaret C., Harry J. Thie, Jefferson P. Marquis, Kevin Brancato, Roland J. Yardley, and Clifford M. Graf II, *Outside the Fleet: External Requirements for Navy Officers*, Santa Monica, Calif.: RAND, MR-1472-NAVY, 2001.

Hearings, House of Representatives, Committee on Armed Services, Investigations Subcommittee, Washington, D.C., May 1, 1987.

Joint Chiefs of Staff, *Joint Officer Management*, JCS Admin Pub 1.2, Washington, D.C., June 30, 1989.

_____, *Joint Vision 2010—America's Military: Preparing for Tomorrow*.

_____, *Joint Vision 2020—America's Military: Preparing for Tomorrow*.

Kent, Glenn A., Edward L. Warner III, and David Ochmanek, *Campaign Strategies, CONEMPs, and CONEXs: A Framework for Planning*, Santa Monica, Calif.: RAND, DRR-2629-AF, 2001.

Kirby, Sheila Nataraj, and Harry J. Thie, *Enlisted Personnel Management: A Historical Perspective*, Santa Monica, Calif.: RAND, MR-755-OSD, 1996.

Kostiuk, Peter F., *Research Memorandum: The Navy Manpower-Requirements System*, Alexandria, Va.: Center for Naval Analyses, CPM 87-114, August 1987.

Lewis, David, "DD-21: Another Seawolf?" *Proceedings*, Vol. 127, No. 8, August 2001, pp. 54–57.

Lockman, Robert F., *Trends and Issues in U.S. Navy Manpower*, Alexandria, Va.: Center for Naval Analyses, 1985.

Marcus, Alan J., *Improving Internal Navy Allocation Decisions: The Case of Military Manpower*, CRM 95-222.10, Center for Naval Analyses, May 1996.

Maze, Rick, "Lawmakers Reluctantly Endorse Joint Duty Waivers," *Air Force Times*, August 30, 1993, p. 9.

National Defense Research Institute, *Results of Pilot Survey of Potential Joint Duty Positions*, Santa Monica, Calif.: RAND, PM-205-JS, February 1994.

Naval Research Advisory Committee, *Optimized Surface Ship Manning*, Arlington, Va., April 2000.

_____, *Executive Summary: Optimizing Surface Ship Manning*, Arlington, Va., April 2000. Available at http://nrac.onr.navy.mil/webspace/exec_sum/99op_man.html (last accessed August 7, 2002).

Navy Manpower Analysis Center, *Navy Total Force Manpower Requirements Handbook*, Millington, Tenn., April 2000.

"Navy Plans Organizational Changes to Enhance Network Centricity," *Inside the Navy*, October 29, 2001, p. 1.

Office of the Assistant Secretary of Defense (Force Management and Personnel), *Report on the Study of Joint Officer Management Initiatives*, draft, April 1990.

_____(Administration and Management), *Workforce Management*, Department of Defense, Administrative Instruction No. 53, June 26, 2000.

Parcell, Ann D., Donald J. Cymrot, and Carol S. Moore, *The Officer Structure in the 21st Century*, CRM D0003570.A2/Final, Alexandria, Va.: Center for Naval Analyses, May 2001.

Rostker, Bernard, Harry Thie, James L. Lacy, Jennifer H. Kawata, and S. W. Purnell, *The Defense Officer Personnel Management Act of 1980: A Retrospective Assessment*, Santa Monica, Calif.: RAND, R-4246-FMP, 1993.

Ryan, Paul J., "New U.S. Fleet Forces Command," *Proceedings*, Vol. 127, No. 10, October 2001, p. 104.

Savage, Dennis M., *Joint Duty Prerequisite for Promotion to General/Flag Officer*, Carlisle Barracks, Pa.: U.S. Army War College, March 24, 1992.

Schank, John F., Harry J. Thie, and Margaret C. Harrell, *Identifying and Supporting Joint Duty Assignments: Executive Summary*, Santa Monica, Calif.: RAND, MR-622-JS, 1996.

Senate Armed Forces Committee, "Joint Officer Personnel Policy" and "Joint Duty Credit for Equivalent Duty in Operations Desert Shield/Desert Storm," from *the National Defense Authorization Act for Fiscal Year 1994*, Washington, D.C., July 27, 1993.

Stewart, George, Scott M. Fabbri, and Adam B. Siegel, *JTF Operations Since 1983*, Alexandria, Va.: Center for Naval Analyses, CRM 94-42, July 1994.

Surface War Library, "Offshore Warriors: Navy's Surface Combatants Set for More Significant Role in Future Joint-Service Operations Overseas," Available at http://surfacewarfare.nswc.navy.mil/n86/lib_offshore_warriers.html (last accessed August 7, 2002).

Syllogistics, Inc., *Analysis of Current and Alternative Provisions of Title IV: Joint Officer Personnel Policy*, May 1989.

Thie, Harry J., Margaret C. Harrell, and Robert M. Emmerichs, *Interagency and International Assignments and Officer Career Management*, Santa Monica, Calif.: RAND, MR-1116-OSD, 1999.

Tomlinson, Paul L., "How Joint Officer Management Legislation Is Dividing Our Officer Corps," *Marine Corps Gazette*, Vol. 78, No. 10, October 1994, pp. 25–31.

Troshinsky, Lisa, "Navy Creates Full-Time Informational Professional Billets," *Navy News & Undersea Technology*, November 5, 2001, p. 3.

Under Secretary of Defense (Personnel and Readiness), *Joint Duty Assignment Study (Interim Report)*, June 1994.